YOU!

ARE RESPONSIBLE FOR YOUR LIFE!

Open the Way to a Higher Understanding
Of Spirituality, Philosophy, Religion and
YOU!

By: LAWRENCE R. MATHEWS J.D., B.B.A.
(Anpu Waset)

11435 West Buckeye Road, #104-202
Avondale, AZ 85323
623-643-9048
lawrencermathews@msn.com
www.helloworld.com/AnpuWaset

Published by LAWRENCE R. MATHEWS

The author is available for lectures and may be reached at the address above.

ISBN 0-9786346-0-8

YOU!

ARE RESPONSIBLE
FOR YOUR LIFE!

What do we do when we realize that all those things that looked so good at one time- money, fame, the person of our dreams-do not bring complete fulfillment?

"SEEK THE ANSWER TO THE QUESTION WHO AM I"

*"Do Not Allow What You Think,
Or The Way You Think To
<u>Limit</u>
What You Think,
Or The Way You Think!"*

-By: Anpu Waset

*This book is for everyone who questions
The **idea** that living the American Dream
Is all there is to life.*

YOU! ARE RESPONSIBLE FOR YOUR LIFE!

TABLE OF CONTENTS

SECTION I

SECTION II

SECTION III

Author's Foreword

There are many today who advocate practices which lead a person to live life more spiritually. More and more people are gravitating towards spiritual practices and moving away from religious ones. These people use the phrase *"we are spiritual beings having a human experience."* A phrase that I believe is true.

The *idea* about life, its purpose, and how it is to be lived was much different in the eras preceding European/white/western domination and rule.

In what is today referred to as northern Uganda, Sudan and Ethiopia once lived a great African people who moved north and settled in what they called Kemet. (The Black land or the land of the Blacks.) The name Kemet was later referred to as Egypt by the Greeks who would later study in this land under the tutelage of their Sages. These black Africans built a civilization that was/is the progenitor of all cultures that have come after it. The great Temples, the Sphinx and the Pyramids to name a few even today confound and baffle the so-called experts of the world.

The *idea* about life and its purpose from the African perspective exemplified the *idea* that people are *spiritual being having a human experience.* The entire culture was based upon this way of thought. This *idea* about life and its purpose allowed Kemet to become one of the greatest civilizations the Earth has ever known. Unfortunately over time, this *idea* gave way to the present eat, drink and be merry mindset which is prevalent today.

This book is written for those people of today who believe that *" we are spiritual beings having a human experience."* This book was written to show people how to identify unconscious practices which interfere and impede upon a person's ability to live life spiritually. If we actually are spiritual beings having a human experience, then the ***reality*** is that we are ***"spirit"*** not flesh. However, many people don't "see" or "live" their lives from this spiritual perspective. They "see" themselves as human. They "live" their lives as humans. For many the following phrase is actually what is "practiced." *"People are human beings having intermittent spiritual experiences."* Very few live their life from the perspective that they are actually spirits or from the spiritual aspect of their nature. Even those of us striving to live spiritually still battle with the underlying recurrent idea that we are human.

What is it that makes many people believe they are something (human) which they are not? Science has told us since 5th grade science classes that everything at its base is composed of atoms a.k.a. energy, a.k.a. spirit. However the uncontested reality of the science makes little if any impact on our beliefs of who we are. What is happening that keeps us from being able to fully "realize" the "reality" of who we are?

It is our **<u>"IDEAS."</u>** People do not know what ideas are and what they are not. Many people do not know how the so-called reality of an idea colors the perception of all of our experiences. It is the belief in a multitude of mistaken ideas that promote and sustain the so-called reality that we are human beings. It is this same belief that makes us ignorant of who we are innately.

In this work a systematic way of identifying **ideas** is presented that keeps people ignorant of realizing the uncontested reality of who they are. This way of "seeing" life prevents a person from being able to answer the age old question, "Who Am I?" This way also prevents a person from being able to take absolute control of their life. First, you are shown how to identify your mistaken **ideas.** Then you are shown the conscious and unconscious practices which reinforce the mistaken **ideas**. Upon completion of the book, you will have the first set of tools necessary to begin the process of "cleansing" your mind of ideas which keep you ignorant of the higher "subtle" aspect of yourself. A process which when completed allows you to FULLY REALIZE the truth behind the phrase, *"we are spiritual beings having a human experience."*

FOREWORD

We are responsible for our life! What an important idea. One might say that upon this concept rests a person's capacity to successfully traverse the murky waters of life or succumb to the sufferings or pitfalls and failures of a life that otherwise could have been well lived. But what is the difference between an idea and reality, empowerment or weakness, good luck and bad luck? How can a person find a way to the power of self-determination and spiritual evolution? How to avoid the pitfalls of life or at least learn from mistakes in order to avoid them in the future and move on to lead a positive and fruitful life?

This book is a lucid discourse on the proper meaning of life and how to live life well; how to understand feelings and ideas, our own or those of others, be they incorrect or correct and how they control our lives. One of the keys presented in this book is understanding how to look at the world and our being and how we allow the ideas we learned about the world to control our lives and lead us away from living a meaningful and successful life. If we accept that we have the capacity to control our lives and if we realize that we are responsible for our life then we need to understand what life is about and how to take that control.

Anpu skillfully explains, through personal experiences, philosophy, and spiritual wisdom based on years of reflection and personal as well as formal spiritual researches, the means for taking that control and how to think about the world in a way that is empowering. This book is an easy to understand exposition of many advanced psychological and philosophical concepts placed in a context of spiritual awakening and practical life situations. It demonstrates how the obstacles one confronts in life can be overcome if one is determined to accept responsibility for one's life and the desire to be free from one's own complicity in the creation of one's own present conditions. Those are high goals for most people and they require patience and courage the means to which he illustrates in this book.

Thus, this book is highly recommended not just for those who may find themselves in negative conditions of life. It is also useful for those who would like to understand the meaning of life and the practical application of advanced spiritual and philosophical concepts imparted by the great sages. It is a valuable and useful volume which will be welcomed by all lovers of truth, seekers of meaning in life and those who study psychology, spirituality and philosophy as a means to understand and discover real and abiding love, peace and spiritual enlightenment in life. Therefore, I am very pleased to write this foreword and to receive this volume into the ranks of altruistic and beneficial literatures of the world which add wisdom and sanity as well as spiritual awakening to our world.

–Dr. Muata Ashby
4/22/2007

Is This Book For Me?

It is no surprise that more and more people are thinking about the purpose of life. After growing from childhood to adulthood—most of us working, marrying, and having children—many North Americans still yearn for something more. They see that after about 70 years or so, death arrives; for far too many of us, little of real value is gained over those years.

Even if you make a lot of money, financial success can't go with you after death. What you leave behind is a greater legacy than wealth: the people who you loved, their memories of you, and your accomplishments. What you take with you are your own unfulfilled desires.

This book is for everyone who questions the **idea** that living 'The American Dream' is all there is to life. Many of us are increasingly frustrated with the ways of the world, and are searching for something more. But do we have to go meditate on a mountain to find that 'something more'? What do we do when we realize that all those things that looked so good at one time—money, fame, the person of our dreams—do not bring complete fulfillment?

Sometimes, people are not aware that they are questioning the American Dream. How often do you think or feel any of the following:

How come I'm lonely?
Why am I not attractive?
Why am I always sick?
How come I can't lose weight?
Why am I always tired/sad?
Why don't I have friends?
Why don't I understand my wife/husband?
Why can't I find someone who will love me for me?

Everyone has tough days, but when these sorts of thoughts come up again and again, it may be a sign of someone who is unconsciously questioning how they choose to live. These statements of frustration are born out of the **IDEA** about life to bring complete fulfillment.

We have all asked ourselves the question "Who Am I?" Have you actively pursued finding the answer to the question? Do you have absolute control of yourself? If not, do you want to take absolute charge and control of your life?

If you identify with anything you have just read, then this book is for you. Let me show you ways of asking those questions that will help you find some of the answers. Along the way, you will discover paths to a new understanding of what is happiness and fulfillment in life.

Obstacles

Successful people accept the premise that a person is <u>completely</u> responsible for the present circumstance in their life. But many people believe that fate or luck is what got them into their current condition. This belief in fate or luck is a way of thinking based on 'victimhood'. I use 'victimhood' in this book to describe a person **who is at the effect of circumstances.** In other words, they hand off responsibility for their successes and failures: *I couldn't help it—I was just lucky/unlucky.* This is different from consciously **creating** their circumstance.

Of course, there are always things that happen—tragedies and losses—that are beyond your control. But how you act and react in those situations is part of **creating** your circumstances. You can remain in the blame mode of 'victimhood'. Or you can take the most dreadful of circumstances, find your inner strengths, and go forward.

We all have a bit of this 'victimhood' mentality inside us, but it is how much is present that differs. Sometimes, we do not even realize that this mentality is present. Many of us become stuck in the way we think and rely on saying "That's just the way I am!" It is an easy out, but it only serves to block us from recognizing our role in our present circumstances. "That's just the way I am" is an obstacle to happiness and fulfillment.

Obstacles are mistaken ideas that become real or true in our mind. **Ideas** that are no longer questioned. **Ideas** that are not true. **Ideas** that color our view of reality.

We all have **'ideas'** about a variety of things—**ideas** about what is happiness, joy, anger, the American Dream, love, forgiveness, peace, money, success and many others. People live their lives in accordance with these **ideas** and accept them as true. However, many of these are **ideas** which will not stand the test of time. It is more probable than not that in 5, 10, 20, or even 100 years, the **idea** you were so sure of today will be found to be false.

For example, there was a time everyone believed in the **idea** that the world was flat. That **idea** today is ridiculous but for centuries, the belief in a flat world was not even questioned. It was accepted as a 'universal truth' and everything people did in thinking about the shape of the world—from travel to geography to science—was based on this mistaken **idea**.

For 15th century citizens, this 'flat world' **idea** was an **obstacle** towards their ability to see life in a different way. How different our world would be if Christopher Columbus hadn't challenged that mistaken **idea**.

When you stop questioning the truth of an idea, you soon forget that it was only an idea. Once accepted as truth, the **idea** becomes '**real**' in the mind. Belief in the so-called **"reality"** of an **idea** which is mistaken creates an impediment to identifying with the phrase, *"we are spiritual beings having a human experience."*

"That's just the way I am" shows up in your thinking and conversation after you grab hold of an **idea** and make it reality. Holding on tight to the **idea** is what makes the **idea** an obstacle to personal growth and self-discovery. When you give away the right to be open to different **ideas** you may not realize that *your right to choose has been given away!*

This book explores society's common **ideas** about the following topics:

- personal responsibility
- love
- happiness
- nutrition
- forgiveness

When you think about love, are your beliefs and actions shaped by what you have been told about 'love' or by what you have actually observed? How did you choose your **ideas** of what love is in the first place? Did you make a conscious choice to accept the present societal views on love? Or did you unknowingly accept it?

Many people have grown up thinking that having a lot of money is the means to success. For them, climbing the corporate ladder and earning lots of money is the American Dream. The cost of this success does not matter. Whether you have to spend long periods of time away from home or that your children grow up without knowing you, or that your relationships falter—none of this matters as long as you achieve 'success'.

We have accepted this **idea** of success for a long time. We are now beginning to see that this **idea** was *mistaken.*

Less than one hundred years ago, doctors performed surgery on patients without sterilizing their instruments. They used the same surgical instruments over and over again. In fact, they did not even wash their hands prior to the surgeries. No one thought it was necessary. Doctors were surprised to complete successful surgeries only to have their patients get sick or die from "unknown reasons". The **idea** of "unknown reasons" turned out to be infection from bacteria and germs on the tools and hands. The **idea** of the "unknown reason" was a mistaken **idea**.

The common denominator about mistaken **ideas** is that they will not stand the test of time. It may take one hundred years, or it may only take a year or months, but eventually **ideas** change as people continue growing, evolving, and learning more about life and the world around them.

Do you allow your **ideas** to change as you change? Will your **ideas** about personal responsibility, love, happiness, nutrition and forgiveness—the topics expressed in this book—stand the test of time? Or will future generations find today's **idea** about their practice to be archaic and backwards like how we find the people of Columbus's time? If your present **ideas** on these topics will not stand the test of time, should you base your outlook on life on an **idea** that is not true?

Living your life—making decisions and acting in certain ways that are based on believing an **idea** that is untrue means that you are living your life based on an ***illusion!***

What Is Meant By *Living A Spiritual Life?*

For the purpose of this book, the word 'spiritual' means any attempt to help us understand those ultimate life questions: *Who am I?* and *what's life all about?* Whatever you do that leads you to the answer of either of these questions is simply you being engaged in living a spiritual life. So spirituality may—or may not—be related to organized religion. In fact, most of today's organized religions do not look for an answer to the question "Who Am I?"

Recognize How You Can Avoid Obstacles
And Live a Spiritual Life

The YOU book is written to help you understand how certain obstacles make it hard for you to answer the question "Who Am I?" A question when answered which helps a person consciously identify with the phrase, *"I am a spiritual being having a human experience."* These obstacles are just **ideas** that color our concept of reality. If **ideas** that are not true form the foundations for how your life is lived, then you are probably living in a world of fantasy and illusion. It is this world of false **ideas** that frustrates and disappoints us again and again. It is also this world that has us believe that we are something (human) other than what we are. (spirit)

Each chapter in this book explores a specific obstacle to living a spiritual life.

Pay attention to the word "Recognize" in this section's title. This book was designed to bring awareness to you about specific obstacles/**ideas**. The book will not teach you how to rid yourself of obstacles. Even if you find that some of the topics offer tips and techniques to remove obstacles, this book is just the first step. People have **ideas** about so much in the world around them. Identifying the many areas in which your reality is colored by mistaken **ideas** will take time. But once you identify those different areas, then you will be ready for the next step. Therefore, a more detailed process will be saved for another time. First, you need to develop a deeper awareness of your obstacles. Then you will be in a position to do something about them.

The best part of this process is that you will discover that you begin to lose those obstacles as you become aware of each one. You will start being attracted to "material" that did not interest you before. You will notice things about life that you missed. And best of all, you will be drawn to circumstances and situations that will allow you to go deeper into your search for the answer to life's ultimate question.

Ultimately, you will recognize the following:

- Your present **idea** about each topic;

- Whether or not this **idea** will stand the test of time, or will what you "know" today be rejected as untrue 100, 50, 25, 5 or 1 year from now?
- And most importantly, you will become aware of who made the decision to adopt the **idea** in the first place.

In other words, you will learn to recognize if you accepted the **idea** as truth after careful thought and reflection—or did you accept this **idea** because everyone else accepted it as the standard?

When you understand that much, you will be in a position to recognize your role in accepting **ideas** about the many subjects in the book. And you will make decisions based on your new understanding of how life is to be lived.

No more living your life based upon some old and tired **idea** that is "just the way it is".

How to Read the Book

This may not be an easy book to read, but it is a book that can help make you free from old **ideas** and obstacles that keep you tied to unhappy life patterns. As you read on, you may notice that some of my concepts will not be accepted by your ego/personality. That's okay. The negative voice you hear in the back of your head is the ego/personality of the 'you' who identified with the present **idea**. So you may find some disagreement with yourself. Consider reading only one chapter per day to allow you time to absorb and work through the inner debate.

Thinking about the points in each chapter is an important tool to unlock your new awareness. After reading a chapter, try to spend a least fifteen minutes reflecting on what you discovered about yourself. Reflect on how the subjects you explored fit into your current life, and what you might like to change.

The book is written in three sections:

SECTION 1 – **OBSTACLES** – explores our **ideas** only. **Ideas** that a person now accepts as *reality*. The **idea**s (chapters) on personal responsibility, love, happiness, nutrition, and forgiveness are included in this section.

SECTION II – **WAYS OF BEING** – explores 'what' people do on a daily basis, and 'how' they 'see' themselves. Ways of Being is the foundation of what we 'practice' daily, and reinforces the so-called reality of an **idea**. Like the bread of a sandwich, ways and practices hold together our **idea,** whether or not the **idea** is valid or an illusion.

SECTION III – **OBSTACLES & WAYS OF BEING** – focuses on "relationships", specifically the Obstacles and Ways of Being in male/female relationships. This last section shows you how your present **ideas** about relationships can set you up to fail from the beginning. No matter how long you are together, if your common present **ideas** about relationships are based on illusions, your relationships will never reach emotional honesty and complete fulfillment.

"Do Not Allow What You Think,
Or The Way You Think To
<u>Limit</u>
What You Think,
Or The Way You Think!"

-By: Anpu Waset

SECTION I

OBSTACLES?

Obstacles are **ideas** about life that you accept as true. You 'forget' that the **idea** started out as an 'opinion' or 'thought' and you now believe that it is true. The **idea** has now become your reality. Now you have obstacles instead of **ideas** because you identify the **idea** as real. This so-called 'reality' leaves no room in your mind for any other **idea** or possibility.

Before Christopher Columbus sailed for the New World, people thought he was crazy because of the belief that the world was flat. This flat-world **idea** was not true—but people accepted this **idea** as real and acted in accordance with this mistaken belief. No one dared sail too far in case they fell off the edge of the Earth. Almost everyone thought Columbus was crazy.

The flat-world **idea** was an **idea** about a tangible object. But people also get **ideas** about things that are not tangible. For example, the idea that a child should grow up with both parents in the home is an **idea** that is in the mind. You can't touch it or hold it in your hands. But how you accept an **idea** in the mind is no different than how you accept a tangible one. A child with this **idea** may grow up with self-esteem issues because most people accept and adopt this **idea** in the mind about both parents. Eventually, this **idea** can be the way that kids from single-parent families come to believe that they have missed out in life. Hurt then develops because of the **idea** that they have missed out. With a different **idea**—a different reality—nothing would have been missed, hence, there would be no basis for hurting. A different **idea** such as "Growing up with one parent was just what it was, and I'm a stronger person because….", OR "Coming from a single-family home gave me just one parent to focus on…"

So an **idea** becomes an obstacle once a person accepts that the **idea** is true and reality-based. In this person's mind the **idea** has stopped being an **idea** and is now reality. In the case of the child, the idea that both parents should raise him/her stops being an **idea** and becomes real. The newly created reality creates the pain and sorrow that often soon follows.

22

The chapters in this section are a small number of obstacles that are common to many of us. Things seen today as 'reality' were once only new **ideas**—concepts that are in fact still only *IDEAS*!

CHAPTER 1

YOU Are Responsible For Your Life!
(Personal Responsibility)

REFLECTION:

1   What Is YOUR present *Idea* about personal responsibility?
2   Where did the *Idea* come from?
3   Did YOU consciously adopt this *Idea*?
4   Is the *Idea* true?
5   Will your *Idea* stand the test of time?

You can trace your present circumstance—your lot in life—directly to a previous action and previous actions done by you in the past. This means that your reactions—how you chose to respond to any situation—your behaviors are a large part of the reason for your present circumstance. Even under the most dreadful conditions, you can keep control of your life by controlling how you choose to react. By controlling your reactions, you empower yourself to control your life!

The **idea** that you are responsible for all of your present circumstances is empowering. This **idea** allows you to make changes in your life. Many people do not share this **idea**.

Most people seem to believe the **idea** that things happen in our lives for no reason, good or bad. In other words, you have good luck when things go well and bad luck when they do not. This meek and passive response creates a condition—a state of living life—in which you are always 'at the effect of the world' instead of becoming in control of it through your response to life's ups and downs.

Let me give you an example. There was once a young man who was told by a friend that if he dug a hole right next to his home he would eventually find a pot of gold. His friend was mistaken when he told him to dig at this particular location, but neither of them knew this.

Well, the young man wanted to be rich so of course he began to dig. He thought all along that eventually he would find this pot of gold and all of his cares and worries would be solved. Next to the side of his house, he dug and dug almost without stopping, continuing for hours and then days and then weeks.

After a couple of months, another one of his friends saw him digging and told him that his other friend had been mistaken, that there was not in fact gold beneath the house. However, by now the young man was so caught up in the **idea** of being rich that he did not believe this new account. He kept on digging anyway.

Before he knew it, he had dug so deep and long next to his home that the foundation gave way. The next thing he knew, his home caved in and he barely escaped.

How many areas of your life are there where you have been sold a bill of goods? How often have you been mistakenly told one thing, believed it and then this mistaken **idea** causes you a great deal of angst, frustration, and upset? How often have you believed the **idea** of someone else and the same thing happened?

One of the things that North American society tells people is that having a lot of money will make you happy. You just have to look at the happy, carefree people driving new cars and wearing the latest fashion in television and print ads to recognize that **idea**. But does money give you happiness? We all know the answer is no. Consider the self-destructive behavior among the wealthy: addictions, divorce and plastic surgeries are not signs of happiness.

So this is a mistaken **idea**, just like a pot of gold underneath the man's house was a mistaken **idea** as well. For many of us even though we know that money doesn't create happiness, this knowledge is only on the surface. It is said with the mouth, but it is not believed within. Inside many of us is the quiet belief that if we had more money, we would be happy. So we act in one of the following ways: doing things that will get us money no matter the consequences on ourselves, or society. Or we carry on living life, all the time feeling deprived that we are missing out on something because we aren't rich, or rich enough.

Either way—doing anything for money, or doing nothing but feeling like a loser without lots of money—it's no different from the man who kept on digging for the treasure even when he was told that it wasn't there.

When You Recognize Your Mistake, You Will Turn Your Life Around

Reflect on the following. What happened to the hole that the man was digging while he continued to dig? It kept getting bigger and deeper. His situation got worse. So your circumstance will only get worse as long as you continue acting in accordance with a mistaken belief.

I remember that I grew up thinking that as long as a person lived, they would always have bills. So I tended to spend money that I did not have. I was using my credit cards even when I couldn't pay it back the next month. I borrowed money instead of saving it. All in the name of 'living' since I was always going to have bills.

It didn't take long for me to accumulate quite a debt. It got so bad that I ended up without enough credit to enjoy 'living' life anymore. I wound up not being able to afford living at all. Granted I couldn't afford it before as I was borrowing money to pay for things, but once everything was maxed out, it seemed like my living was over. However, a strange thing happened to me at different points in my life.

Every time I got too far in debt, I wound up getting a higher paying job. Now you would think that this would be a time that I would start clearing up this spending habit with the extra money I had. No, I did not. Instead, I used the extra money for me and continued making minimum payments and continued borrowing using credit. It's really true that old habits die hard.

One day I woke up and realized that the financial hole I had dug was now just too big. Fortunately I realized this before my house (and other areas in my life) caved in altogether.

So you see, it's easy to believe a mistaken **idea**, live in to that mistaken **idea**, and wind up getting in a large hole—and not even realize it until it's too late.

The inability to recognize your personal responsibility in your life's present circumstance is an obstacle to answering the question "Who Am I?" Did the man digging for the gold have time to work on this spiritual aspect of his life? He may have thought about it, but what were his actions? His actions were actions of digging. The digging took time and even though he may have thought about practices which would lead to the discovery of the answer "Who Am I", what he was doing was in fact digging. And, at the end of the night, he was probably too tired from digging to spend time on the spiritual aspect of his life. After his home caved in, he wouldn't have time to concentrate on this aspect of life because by then he had to find another home to live in.

For me, I was living or doing what I could do to get by not worrying about bills since they were always going to be there. At the time I went to church, and even though I was active in it, my actions were in accord with 'living' and enjoying life. By the time I realized what happened, I accumulated so much debt that it took me a long time to get rid of it.

In fact, my 'hole' had become so large that it's still taking a great deal of time and effort to fill it in. All this effort has left little time or energy for practicing those things that allow me to be in harmony with nature and the spiritual aspect of me.

We all dig holes for ourselves most often because of mistaken **ideas** that we act in accordance with. In essence, we don't know any better. In this environment, there is little energy or room left for delving into the spiritual aspect of one's being.

YOU Are The Cause Of Your Present Life's Circumstance!

This book is designed to help you recognize that your present circumstance is a direct result of previous actions done by you. Therefore, **YOU** are the cause of your present life's circumstance. This should be encouraging to know. This means that whatever situation you have brought yourself to, you can bring yourself out of it. This relates to the Law of Cause and Effect. This law in essence means that for every cause placed into the universe, there will be an equal effect. Now this does not mean that the way the law works will be identical for each of us. For example, if you give a homeless person $10 dollars today it doesn't mean that someone will give you $10 dollars tomorrow. It means that the energy—the thought—behind the giving will go into the universe and it is that energy/thought that will come back to you.

If you take time to study the natural world—the planets, animals etc.—you will notice a regularity to it. You can see in life and in the heavens that everything is circular. Seasons occur at the same intervals every year. The moon travels around the Earth in a circle, and the Earth does the same around the sun. The sun itself circles around the Milky Way galaxy in a circle. People often say "what goes around comes around."

We do not realize the full extent of this universal principle in our own life. Too often we attribute the 'good things' in our life as good luck or a blessing. Just as we often assign so-called 'bad things' to life as bad luck and a woe-is-me victim type of mentality (remember 'victimhood'?) The **ideas** about our fortune seem to happen outside of ourselves and our input. Therefore these **ideas** reinforce the **idea** that we are a victim of our circumstance. A victim of life. This internal **idea** of being a victim occurs regardless of the so-called good occurrence or so-called bad one.

A victim is 'one at the effect of something or someone'. In both instances, we believe that things happen to us outside of our input.

However, according to nature and how life operates, this **idea** could not be further from the truth. If the law of cause and effect is true, then your present circumstance is the direct result of your previous actions, previous thoughts, and previous **ideas**. Through a previous thought and action, you have created your blessing. Through a previous thought and action you have created your misfortune.

I believed from the time I was young that there would always be bills. Consequently I later had a lot of bills. Unfortunately modern religion makes the problem worse by teaching us that we don't have to accept responsibility for ourselves and our actions. It is taught that "someone" will save us from our actions. It is not taught to live life in accordance with the principles that this 'someone' lived by. Living life in accordance with these principles gives us the power to fix those aspects of our lives that keep us in a state of victimhood.

Someone may save you one day. However, until that happens, you want your body and mind to be in tip-top shape.

If you have high blood pressure, stop eating greasy foods. If you are overweight, stop eating chocolate sundaes and cakes and get some exercise. If you drink when you get frustrated, eat a piece of fruit when the desire occurs. Do something that will be good for you instead of that which causes you to dig your hole deeper.

You also want your life, and household to be free of worry and frustration. A savior will not stop you from that cake. You have to do that. A savior will not stop you from having that drink. You have to do that. A savior did not get my finances in order. I had to do that myself.

Until you accept responsibility for your present circumstance in life, you will not be able to live a spiritual life. You may think you are, but in reality you aren't because you don't have the time or energy to devote to the spiritual practice. You are, in fact, digging a hole for yourself and your time is actually being spent digging or looking for a new house after yours caves in.

How many different areas are there in your life where you're digging holes? Finances? Relationships? Looking for happiness? Many people are digging holes for themselves in many different areas of their lives. It's not just one. Have you ever known someone who got involved in a relationship to be happy and less than a year later they were miserable and now also had a child and more bills? All for the sake of happiness.

Create A New Future By
Being Different In The Present

So for today, erase the **idea** that your life is something that happens *to* you. You are the creator of your present, and you will create your future by consciously choosing certain actions and **ideas** that will bring you to the future you want. There's a lot of power in this **idea.**

YOU are in control of your life. You do have free will. But how are you going to exercise this will? Always remember the law of cause and effect. If you begin today to do only those actions that are peaceful, contented, and full of love, care and concern for yourself, family, others, and the world, you'll create a tomorrow for yourself that will hold those same qualities.

Remember that what goes around does come back around. Begin today by no longer digging holes in your life. You do this yourself. You don't need anyone's help to stop. YOU are a child of the Divine (God), so start acting like it. With that type of power, self-control should be easy. Do you really believe that you're a child of the Divine (God)?

If more people really believed that they were children of the Divine (God), controlling themselves would be much easier. No one is asking you to walk on water, or to feed thousands of people with a couple of fish. Just become a calm person with self control and you won't create holes that keep you so busy that you have no time to focus on the spiritual aspects of your life.

It takes practice to learn self-control, but this practice will lead you to a different type of life. You will actually begin to take control of your life. And it gets better. You will become physically healthier because you will begin eating food that is proper fuel for the body. You will become mentally healthier because you will stop digging holes and begin filling them up.

In the beginning, you won't notice a real difference as you fill those holes since it takes as much energy to put dirt back into the ground as it did to take it out. But soon enough the hole will fill in, and as you see it fill, you will begin to start feeling better. Better because as this hole is filled, this will be one less thing to worry about as you eliminate a cause of stress in your life.

Before you know it, you will fill all of the holes that you dug previously, and you will be left with a life which allows you to be happy, joyous, peaceful and contented. This is a wonderful feeling and a wonderful way to live life.

With all the baggage cleared out of your life, your time and energy can be directed and focused on discovering and then experiencing the higher ideals in life. Experiencing ourselves as spirits having a human experience. You need space to do this and filling in the holes in your life will allow this to occur.

YOU are responsible for your reaction to your present life circumstance. YOU are not a victim of anything. YOU create tomorrow's blessing or tomorrow's bad luck based upon YOUR response to life's present situation.

What is YOUR present **idea** about your contribution to your present circumstance? Is it an **idea** that you chose? Or is it an **idea** adopted from mainstream society? Is it an **idea** that is true? Will this same **idea** be around in 20 years, 10 years, and 1 year? Or will it also be ridiculed in time like that of the world being flat?

The ability to control the response to situations is an idea that gives you power. An African Kemetic proverb captures it so well: "Emotions are good servants but poor masters."

Many of us react to situations in the same automatic way—a reaction based on a specific emotion that we have become used to in other similar situations. This way of living (reacting to life) is an **idea** that does not empower you. In fact, it limits your power and strength. It is an **idea that will not stand the test of time**!

CHAPTER 2

What About Love?
(Love)

REFLECTION:

1   What is YOUR present *Idea* about what constitutes Love?
2   Where did the *Idea* come from?
3   Did YOU consciously choose this *Idea* or was it something adopted based upon societal norms?
4   Is the *Idea* true? Will it stand the test of time?

The Sun in the sky shines continuously.
It shines on those who do good deeds.
It shines on the so-called evildoers.
The Sun does not hold back its rays for any reason.
It does not discriminate.
It gives because that is what it was created to do.
–Anpu Waset

The above is an **idea** about the nature of Love. This **idea** about Love is different from that which is practiced by most of society. In fact this **idea** totally contradicts the kind of Love practiced by many today. A compelling argument can be made that the above **idea** is actually closer to what Love truly is and what it was designed to be. A true love is an **idea** that may actually stand the test of time.

When we speak or think about 'Love' often we think of happy feelings or emotions. These thoughts trigger chemical reactions in our bodies and these chemical reactions are identified by a person as "feeling good." These thoughts may be referred to as "feel-good feelings." These feelings, (a.k.a. Love by mainstream society) are generally associated with a spouse or significant other. People also tie these "feel-good feelings" to other members of their family, such as parents or siblings. Close friends may also be included in the circle of people for which the "feel-good feeling" is allowed to arise. The "feel-good feelings" about those other than your immediate family are generally the same but without the same power. These "feel-good feelings" are what people associate and identify as Love. This is the common prevalent **idea** about Love. Is this really what Love is—a "feel-good feeling" about someone in your immediate family or circle of friends?

Love is Unconditional and
Given Without Expectation

The quote at the beginning of the chapter describes an unconditional Love that is given without expectation. Does your present **idea** about Love allow you to Love unconditionally?

There are evil people in this world who do terrible things. There are also people who allow evil people to do evil things. There are also many who don't directly do bad things, but they are mischievous. They gossip. They talk about others behind their backs. They keep rumors going and create confusion and ill will.

How many people today treat all of those types the same as they treat the people who they say they love? Very few. However, the sun provides its life-giving rays to all. It does not discriminate. It does not withhold its warmth for *any* reason. This is what "Love" truly is: Loving unconditionally; loving without expectation; loving because you yourself have become Love.

Love is a state of being. It is much more than a "feel-good feeling." Love is open and accepting and fully recognizes the oneness behind all of creation. So loving all equally is in actuality what true Love is. A way of being towards others that comes naturally once you have realized the underlying oneness of all of creation.

This way of being, this **idea** of Love where you love all equally, allows many wonderful things to happen. It allows your consciousness to expand. We may think that the world is made of everything that we experience through our five senses—taste, touch, smell, hearing and sight—but there is far more to existence. Expanding your consciousness allows you to become aware of aspects of creation that are subtle and not outwardly apparent. Another wonderful thing that happens with this way of being—loving all without conditions—is that it gets rid of a negative trait from your personality. It helps you eliminate egoism from your personality. Egoism is the belief that self-interest is more important than anything else—if you hold your love based on self-interest and egoism, then you only love when it makes **you** happy or content. This is important because it is egoism that most people today call "Love". This **idea** we have today about Love is not Love.

Love Today Is Reserved for Only a
"Special Class of People"

Many people talk about love and its importance. There are sayings that refer to love throughout the ages—from ancient times to the poets and songwriters of today, love has been and continues to be a popular topic. People place a lot of importance on what we call 'Love'.

But if you really think about it, you can see what we consider to be Love is anything but real love. In fact, what we consider to be love is only given and devoted to a specific and particular class of people or things.

We love our spouse or significant other. We love our children. We love our parents, our siblings, our pets. We even love our country, our cars or clothes or other objects. These are the people and things that are "Loved". These people and things are the "special class" that receives our love.

For everyone and everything else we don't even really care. Not in a mean sense or in the sense in that we wish others harm. But in the sense that those others do not belong to the *"special class of people"* that we have chosen to be Loved by us. Therefore the best that we offer to those outside of our chosen group is tolerance. Others outside of the "special class of people" are treated differently directly and/or indirectly by us. The thought rarely if ever crosses our mind to Love everyone and everything else the same. Oh, we may allow ourselves to "like" others, but our Love is reserved for only the *"special class of people"* in our lives.

When you allow your personality to 'hold back' or reserve Love, you are setting yourself up for dangerous and serious consequences. As I already suggested, reserving Love is actually egoism or self-interest. Egoism should be eliminated not encouraged because it leads to judgment of people which takes on different forms.

With the first form of judgment, you put yourself at a level where you are "better" than others outside of the "special class of people" that you keep your love for—persons not considered to be on that same level. Rarely will you look down on a person within your "special class" no matter what the circumstances. Generally, you reserve this type of judgment for those outside of the group.

Consider the times you have said or thought these types of judgment statements:
- refer to others <u>outside</u> of the "special class" by calling them names:
  Those guys are bums.
  Look at that lazy person.
  They're nothing but a bunch of terrorists.

Now consider how often you have said or thought these types of judgment statements about people in similar circumstances who also happen to be in your "special class of people":
- refer to a person <u>inside</u> the "special class" by qualifying their circumstances:
  Those guys are just down on their luck.
  That person just hasn't yet figured out what they want to do with their life.
  Why they're just freedom fighters.

Your judgment of others is a case of beauty being in the eye of the beholder.

With the second form of judgment you develop a level of jealously toward those outside your *"special class of people."* When someone outside of your *"special class of people"* says or does things that bring into focus your own feelings of inadequacy, you tend to react by becoming jealous and/or envious. In truth, often many of us don't feel good about ourselves, or at least hold self-esteem issues that we may not even realize we have. But classifying others as a "special class" is a breeding ground for jealousy and envy. All of this leads to the following sad fact: it is rare if ever, that most of us feels good about the good fortune of one outside of our *"special class of people".*

Over time, this **idea** about Love—that you reserve it for your *"special class of people"*—actually leads to the opposite of Love. For most, this **idea** leads to intolerance; for some extreme cases, it leads to hate. This idea also reinforces an unconscious **idea** that others are separate from one another. As long as you think that you are different or separate from others, you will foster distance and separation. The more distant and separate that you think you are, the more likely you are to accept violence and injustice being served on others outside of your group.

In different points of time, and to varying degrees, Africans, Native Americans, the Irish, Italians, and Jews have been kept separate from the *"special class of people"* of those in power. Because they were kept 'separate', violence and injustice were perpetrated and allowed on these groups. This **idea** of others being 'separate' and 'not worthy of our love' allowed such behavior to be acceptable.

Reservation of Love Is an
Obstacle to Living a Spiritual Life

Love that you reserve for only the *"special class of people"* becomes a severe and serious obstacle to you living a spiritual life. You may think that you are practicing Love when in fact you are breeding the opposite. If you aspire to Love based upon the precepts given in your personal religious texts, it can be easy to be led astray when practicing Love.

For example, consider the phrase "God is Love". If you have a reserved "special person classification" system for Love, your **idea** about the meaning of "God is Love" is much different than someone who sees Love as a way of being with all things. Do you think that God is reserved just for you and your special group of people? This sort of thinking also allows you to have an **idea** that all others are un-Godly or heathens because they are outside of the "special class". But if you see Love simply as 'a way of being' and something without condition, your **idea** is much different. It is much deeper and expansive.

This is why the old idea about Love is such an obstacle. A complete and thorough understanding of your religious text will not be possible with **ideas** about Love which did not exist when your specific book of study was written.

Love is Expansive.
It Grows Outward In All Directions.
It Does Not Discriminate.

Is the Love that you practice on a daily basis a type of Love that is expansive? Is it given to all freely? Or is it a restrictive type of Love given to the chosen few? Does the Love that you practice on a daily basis grow outward in all directions? Or does it look more like a single ray which touches a single person or single group of people? Does the Love that you practice everyday discriminate or is it given freely to all? If the Love you practice does not look like this, then you are not actually loving anything. You are actually creating the means by which hate can exist. The means by which intolerance can exist. The means by which injustice can exist. It is an **idea** about Love which may not stand the test of time.

As long as people consider others to be different and classify them as being different, it will be easy to treat others differently. It will be easy to see them differently. It will be easy to apply a different standard to them. To judge them.

Living life in a spiritual way based on spiritual concepts cannot be achieved as long as people have the present **ideas** about Love. Look at the world today. There are many religions. Everyone talks about Love. Everyone says they live based upon Love and its principles. However, leaders of many of the major religions of today won't rest until they convince and convert everyone into their specific set of practices. However, the present **idea** about Love practiced across the religious spectrum has done nothing to combat the ills of the world. It has actually made it worse. There are many today in the religious community who think that it is acceptable to kill others to prepare the way for God. These "others" are always outside of one's *"special class of people."* Killing for any reason is not allowable for

37

any reason in any religion that I have studied. Yet people find reasons to justify it and accept it. Thou Shall Not Kill seems pretty clear on its face. These are the God-fearing people who advocate killing of others. Heads of large churches have outwardly encouraged the assassination of people outside of their *"special class of people"*. What kind of Love is this?

This mindset develops because of the classification of who will and will not receive one's Love. This is not the type of Love talked about in any religious text. It is an **idea** of the 19th and 20th century. God does not have to come down from heaven to make the world a better place. People can Love ALL without discrimination, and I believe that, in as little as five years, the world will change completely. So-called "evil" in the world does not happen as a result of a "devil" or "evil" doer. It is created from a mindset that develops from the present classification system around Love. It is the result of practicing a type of Love that discriminates.

This **idea** is the root of the ills in the world today. A system of Love based upon classification. A Love that is reserved for only a select few.

The verse at the beginning of the chapter is a reflection on what Love really is. The sun shines on all no matter what the circumstance. The sun has MANY reasons to not shine on particular people or places. There are many people who do terrible acts. There are many reasons to hold back its life-giving essence. Almost ALL people Love with conditions! But the sun does not hold back its Love. It shines no matter what. There is no classification of who will receive rays from the sun. All receive life essence *unconditionally.*

Unconditional Love is the type of Love that was spoken of when the writers from all religions wrote their particular book of wisdom. They all were referring to Love which is expansive and grows outward in all directions, infinity. A Love that does not discriminate. A Love that is given to all no matter what they do or no matter what they do not do. A Love which is actually a way of being.

God is in fact Love. A Love that is expansive. A Love that does not discriminate. A Love that is infinite in all directions. When you practice this type of Love everyday, you will become a mini sun. You will be a person who provides life-giving essence to all through kind words or deeds and actions that help the living condition of others. This is what it means to be God-like. The idea that Love is conditional is an **idea** that will not stand the test of time. The world will be a much better place when people adopt a new **idea** about Love. An **idea** that could be that Love is **unconditional** and given to **ALL!**

REFLECTION:

1   **Is the present societal *Idea* about Love true?**
2   **Will this *Idea* stand the test of time?**

CHAPTER 3

HAPPINESS IS.......NOT!
(HAPPINESS)

REFLECTION:

1   What is YOUR present *Idea* about what Happiness is?
2   Where did the *Idea* come from?
3   Did YOU adopt the *Idea* from society's standards?
4   Would YOU like to be happy at all times?
5   Is it possible to be happy at all times?

Is there any person on this planet who does not want to be happy? Everyone wants happiness all of the time and nothing is wrong with this desire. In fact, happiness is something that everyone should and can have continually. However the present common **idea** about happiness does <u>not</u> create the desired state. It actually creates the exact opposite: the conditions of grief, frustration and anxiety. Is this possible? Is it possible that the present **ideas** of what constitutes happiness are in fact the actual cause of unhappiness? This chapter presents a different perspective on **ideas** about happiness. Upon completion of the chapter you will be able to determine if your present **idea** on happiness allows you to have perpetual and continuous happiness—or if it creates the opposite: frustration and sadness.

Before going any further reflect upon the following. What is YOUR present **idea** about what constitutes happiness? Did you choose this **idea** or was it based upon societal standards and norms—something you just accepted without even thinking?

While I wrote this particular chapter of the book, I was in a very happy state. It was that happy state of mind in which no matter what is happening, you easily roll with the punches and are able to swing back even harder. In fact, I recall that I began writing this on a Wednesday night. I also recall smiling a great deal of the time because of my happy state. What took me by surprise while writing was the realization that I had been feeling like this continuously since the previous Friday. With the beginning of the morning of that past Friday up through the following Wednesday night, it was one continuous happy state. For those of you counting, that's six straight days.

As I thought about feeling so good, I thought about what was happening in my life to make me feel this way. There was very little on the outside that would justify this feeling. I had received my lay-off notice so I would soon be unemployed. I had been through some serious relationship issues. I had begun cleaning up some financial issues that I created, and although I was in the process of clearing them up, they were still quite a mess.

From the outside there was nothing that would explain my "happy" state. I was, though, very content. I was also very confident. I knew that no matter how the situation appeared, ultimately it was going to work out. It was a feeling that I couldn't let go even if I wanted to. One of my co-workers called me "optimistic." I guess that was a way of describing it, but that too was a limited way of describing it.

I cannot tell you exactly why I had this feeling for such a long time. Well, at least not yet in this particular book. We will get to that in the next project. But what I will say is that this feeling made me reflect on this society's **idea** of "what happiness actually is." You see, after having this prolonged experience, I began to think that this was in fact the way happiness was meant to be. A continual state of happiness, filled with peace and contentment no matter what is happening around you. I wondered why happiness should be something that occurs intermittently — something that happens occasionally. How come people see happiness from the perspective of occurring haphazardly? Why don't we even think in terms of happiness being something that is a way of life instead of an aspect of life? I ask you: If you thought that it was actually possible to be happy at all times under all conditions, is that something that you would want?

I'm not saying that if you were in car accident *don't worry; be happy*. I'm not saying that I'm happy about being laid off. I'm not saying be happy if a tornado comes through and wipes out your home. What I am saying is that, with practice, you can develop an unshakable type of faith of knowing in the midst of whatever may be occurring that things will be okay. That if you pick up the pieces and begin doing something, the universe will open up and things will come into your space. With this attitude when the universe calls, it normally happens in a much bigger way than what had occurred previously. This happiness state keeps you free to see the opportunity in the midst of the so-called tragedy. It also keeps you in a place where you don't wallow and "wait" for something to happen. You know what happens when you wallow in your emotions and wait for 'rescue'. Things get worse. Not better. The 'happiness state' frees you and allows you to move. It is the movement itself which is the spark plug of the better things to come. You've heard the old adage *you take one step, the Divine will take two.*

I submit to you that our **ideas** about happiness are often what keep us from achieving true happiness. This may sound strange given the fact that ultimately most of us want to be happy. Most, if not all, people claim this as their goal. However, most if not all people "limit" their **idea** about how happiness manifests and how often it can manifest as well.

This "limited" **idea** about what happiness is made of and how it happens is, in fact, an obstacle to living a spiritual life. It is also this "limited" **idea** about how happiness comes to us and what it actually is, that holds you back from achieving a long-term happiness state.

WHAT ARE PEOPLE'S IDEAS ABOUT WHAT CONSTITUTES HAPPINESS?

People's **ideas** about what is happiness, is, in most instances, the root cause of their present and future unhappiness. What are people's **ideas** about happiness and where can they be found? In OBJECTS.

Many people think consciously and unconsciously that they will find happiness in getting objects and things. There are those who think that money will bring them happiness. There are those who think that a home, or a car, or that relationship with that "special one" will do it. You'll recall the earlier **idea** that unconsciously, some people think that objects will bring them joy. This is important to realize because many people will tell you that they know that objects won't bring happiness. But they still strive towards getting a variety of objects—the car, the big house, designer clothes—so they can feel good. So they can be happy.

For now though, recognize that people do not realize that what they consider to be happiness—getting certain objects: people or things—is in fact the cause of a great deal of sadness, anger, grief, stress and heartache. The exact opposite of happiness. To live a spiritual life you must have a peaceful and contented mind. Thinking that you are happy when you are in fact breeding the opposite does not create a peaceful mind. Instead, it creates an agitated or upset mind.

An agitated mind leads to a subtle form of frustration and discontent. Because it is subtle, you don't recognize that it is there. This frustration grows but it doesn't develop into unhappiness. Instead, it manifests as a longing, wanting, or wondering about when things will get better. In this state, you may make statements such as "I deserve better than this" or feel as if you are missing out on something if things don't go your way. This frustration clouds the mind and keeps you in a perpetual subtle state of frustration that grows until the day that it openly manifests. This may be days, weeks, or months, but for most of us, it fully manifests after a period of years.

How many of you have ever thought that a relationship with the "right person" would make you happy? Almost everyone should be raising their hands and saying *Yes! I'm in that club*. Consider my example:

When I was about 8 or 9 years old until I was about 11 or 12, there was a girl in my school named Benita. I thought she was 'the end all and the be all'. She was pretty; she had long hair that I liked. She had a voice that made me melt whenever she spoke to me. She was the smartest girl in the school—at least I thought she was—and I was the smartest boy. At that time she was, to me, simply perfect. I thought that if she was my girlfriend I would be happy. Happiness could be found in a relationship with Benita. Have you ever thought that a relationship with a particular person would make you happy?

But although Benita was always nice to me, she didn't really like me like that. For three or four years I did everything I knew how to do to impress her. I wrote her poems, I would listen to the Motown songs, memorize the song lyrics and say them to her to impress her. I would carry her books if she let me. I did all of these things because I liked her and

43

wanted her to be my girlfriend. In short, my world would be complete; I would be HAPPY if Benita was my girlfriend.

Now let's look at what was going on within me during the 3 to 4 years that I was doing this one-sided courting. First, I wondered how come she didn't like me. I was the smartest boy in my school, and although I was no Denzel Washington, I was also not ugly. So I started wondering about myself. I had to fight the tendency of thinking that something was wrong with me. Every year I actually grew more and more frustrated. Each year I grew more and more disappointed. And each year I was closed off from seeing the other girls who actually did like me. I didn't see them because my eyes were so focused on Benita.

WHAT WAS I ACTUALLY EXPERIENCING DURING THIS TIME?

Now notice something. Within that time period that I courted in vain, inside I was disappointed. I longed to be happy, but in my longing I was actually unhappy and discontent because I felt like I was missing out on something. I thought I deserved better. Has this ever happened to you?

Needless to say I never got that girl. So for the sake of happiness, I wound up wasting 3 to 4 years of time and energy chasing an **idea**. For the sake of happiness, I wound up feeling bad about myself. My **idea** of what would have made me happy, Benita being my girlfriend, was in fact the cause of my frustration and discontent. In my book, frustration and discontent are signs of unhappiness not happiness.

Now let's look further into what was occurring for me during those years that I was attempting to find happiness. Did my **idea** of what would make me happy—Benita being my girlfriend—help move me towards finding happiness? No. It actually had the opposite effect.

Have you ever wanted something that you thought would make you happy and since you didn't have it, you thought you were missing out on something or felt like you deserved it? Recognize that this type of thinking leads to an internal subtle form of discontent and frustration. Did you know that unconscious discontent and frustration leads to argument and many times blame as people begin to blame others—spouses, children, and sometimes even God—for their lot in life? And unfortunately—and this is the most unfortunate—people accept this way of thinking and being as normal, and will not accept it any other way.

Do you see what my **idea** of what Happiness was created for me? The exact opposite of happiness. But I accepted this as being normal as we all do, because that is all that I knew, just like it is all that most of us know. Folks, there is something wrong with this picture.

Now some of you may think that if I had gotten that girl, I would have been happy. But think about your experiences. How long does the "happiness euphoric feeling" last once you get the OBJECT of your affection? Is it permanent?

The reality is that once we get the things (objects) that we create as the means for our happiness, the novelty quickly wears off. We then place another object in that place and the cycle begins again. In the interim there are far longer periods of frustration, discontent, and unhappiness—3 to 4 years in my example—than there are happy periods.

Many of us live in a constant state of discontent and frustration and don't realize it—all for the sake of wanting to happy. Discontent and frustration are brushed aside and treated as normal until you can no longer tolerate the feeling, and then you lash out through your words or actions. You say things that you later regret or unfortunately you lose your temper and you even can become abusive. These feelings can also lead you to using all types of drugs, alcohol included and has people requesting the assistance of psychiatrists and therapy—anything to find relief from the feelings.

Now within this realization comes a great deal to rejoice about. When you come to the full realization of the 'happiness syndrome'—where you first have the euphoric feeling, then over time become frustrated and discontent— you can prevent yourself from letting this rollercoaster ride of emotions take place. However, you first must establish a new **idea.** An **idea** that allows you to believe that Happiness can be achieved at all times.

HAPPINESS CAN BE EXPERIENCED PERPETUALLY

Happiness is in fact something that can be experienced perpetually. In fact, if you haven't learned how to be happy beyond the euphoric-feeling stage, then you are depriving yourself of a natural part of life.

So I know that society's present **ideas** of happiness are actually unnatural. The present **idea** is a mistake. It is an idea which will not stand the test of time. We have learned a false way of living life that leads to much pain and sorrow. Look around you. How far do you have to look to find perpetual happiness? We have yet to recognize that we practice living life in a way that breeds the exact opposite. All we have to do is practice living life in another way and our ability to be happy perpetually will happen.

Practice makes perfect. Anything you practice often you will become good at doing. As a society we practice living life in a way that leads to much unhappiness. When we consciously choose to practice living life in a way that will allow happiness to occur beyond getting objects, we will then free ourselves from the vicious cycle of pain and sorrow. Again it is a way of living life that if practiced will lead one to unending joy and peace.

You don't need another person in your life to make you happy. You can be happy with or without a person. In fact being with a person or obtaining some object has absolutely no bearing on your ability to be happy. This should be the first mode of practice. Developing a new way of thinking which erases the **idea** that you need some type of object to be happy. This will take time, but once mastered, you will then learn how to be happy at all times with yourself. At first it will appear as contentment. Then you will have the actual "happiness state" that I referred to earlier. At least that's what happened to me. If you reflect on what was just said, I think you will see the value in it. Think about it and let your inner self be your guide.
I now know that I will no longer settle for anything less than perpetual happiness. I practice everyday being in the happiness state. This is what people really want. They want happiness ALL OF THE TIME. Not intermittently. No one wants to be hurt and be miserable. People just don't know any other way. Well I'm here to tell you there is another way.

Perpetual happiness is yours when you first understand and accept that there is another way, then practice living your life in accordance with this other way. Accept that this is in fact the way it is supposed to be.

So friends be patient with yourselves. Practice distancing yourselves from the up-and-down folly of society's **ideas** about what constitutes happiness. Become established and rooted in a higher ideal—an ideal that you choose. Never forget that when you live any aspect of life based upon a *mistaken* **idea**, you're living this aspect of life according to an ***illusion***! Do not be like the man who dug the hole with the *mistaken* **idea** that there was treasure underneath the ground. Acting in accordance with this ***illusion*** caused him to make the large hole even larger. It created a mess.

In the realm of happiness, living based upon an ***illusion*** causes you to accept an **idea** that causes pain and sorrow. This too is a mess. You then do the same thing over and over again looking for intermittent moments of happiness. You get far more unhappiness than happiness with this approach. The search for this bliss can lead to hurt feelings, and life choices such as taking on debt or choosing partners on a whim. People's 'holes' just get larger and larger. Is this what Happiness Is? NOT!

REFLECTION:

1   **Would YOU like to be Happy at ALL times?**
2   **Does YOUR present *Idea* about Happiness allow YOU to be Happy at all times?**
3   **If YOUR present *Idea*(s) about Happiness produce intermittent Happiness, is this Idea true?**
4   **Will YOUR present *Idea* on Happiness stand the test of time?**

CHAPTER 4

FOOD FOR THE BODY
FOOD FOR THE MIND,
FOOD FOR THE SOUL.
(NUTRITION)

REFLECTION:

1   Do YOU have an *Idea* about what constitutes proper nutrition?
2   Does this *Idea* include food for the mind and soul?

The present **idea** in society about what is 'proper nutrition' is an obstacle to living a spiritual life. The **idea** from the medical community is that a proper diet means a eating a certain number of foods from the four major food groups. This **idea** assumes that the body is the sum total of the entity known as a "person." This **idea** is untrue, and is an **idea** which will not stand the test of time. There are two other parts that make up the entity known as a "person". They are the mind and the soul. All three parts, the body, mind, and soul make up what we know and call a "person." I know that it's rare to hear someone speak about proper nutrition for the *mind* or *soul*. But healthy food for all three aspects of the "person"—body, mind and soul—is what I call a full and proper nutrition. This is a different **idea** about nutrition from that of mainstream society. I believe that you are malnourished when any one aspect—mind, body, or soul—is not fed properly.

You have probably heard the term "garbage in, garbage out". This also works for nutrition for a "person." It is not possible to live a spiritual life when your body and mind is taking in a variety of poisons and toxins. It is also not possible to understand the subtle aspects of any religious doctrine in this state. Unhealthy food in the body makes the body work harder to rid itself of materials that do not belong. Unhealthy substances prevent your mind from being able to think as it was designed to do. Toxins and poisons create a "cloud" or "veil" over your mind. In this state you can easily fall prey to every whim of the senses. Unfortunately, many of us have taken in a variety of poisons and toxins for so long that we do not realize that our body is not functioning at its best. In other words, everything is okay since you still walk, talk and do a variety of things.

Believe it or not, proper nutrition helps you find answers to those questions "Who Am I" and "Why Am I Here". For self-reflection and studying any religious text, you need to be able to "see" beyond the words. Often, those words have more than one meaning, and have been drafted to appeal to your conscious, subconscious, and unconscious self. As you grow spiritually, your ability to "see" through the words to the deeper meaning of the text should grow as well. So should your ability to apply the teachings to your everyday life.

When your diet is missing a good nutritional content, you will stay at the level of "reading the words only". This deeper meaning will be "hidden" behind the poisons and toxins that cloud your mind. Think of it this way: would regular gasoline in the tank of a car that requires premium unleaded fuel be an obstacle to how well that car works? The car may run for a time, but not at its best, and eventually the car fails to run at all. Improper fuel causes it to fail at a much faster rate. Improper fuel in the Body, Mind and Soul complex does the same thing to you.

When people today speak of proper nutrition, they focus entirely on the body. This type of thinking leads to the whole body/mind/soul complex being malnourished. If you feed your body the proper types of fuel, but feed your mind and senses a lot of junk food, then you are malnourished. The same holds true if you feed your soul the proper type of fuel but feed your body a lot of junk food. And it's the same for the mind: if you feed it junk, it doesn't matter how proper the nutrition is for the body and soul. You need to take care of all three.

As a person is the sum total of his or her parts, (those parts are the body, mind/senses, and soul) then it stands to reason that a problem in any one area leads to problems for the whole. And given that many people do not recognize the significance of their diet for the mind/body/soul, it also stands to reason that many do not bother to feed each the proper fuel.

Feeding yourself a diet based upon the **idea** that you are just a "body" is an **idea** that isn't standing the test of time.

49

This chapter looks more closely at the following:

- First, the three aspects of a person: the body, mind/senses and soul, along with each aspect's role in making up your entire being.
- Each aspect will then individually be discussed with a highlight around the types of food most of us feed that aspect.
- Finally, proper food choices for each aspect will be explored.

BODY, MIND/SENSES, & SOUL COMPLEX

As I said earlier, I believe that each of us is the sum total of our body, mind/senses, and soul. Before thinking about the proper fuel necessary for each aspect, let's explore each aspect individually.

The Body

When you use the word human "body," you often think in terms of the skin and what is inside that skin. As we know from our public school science class, the skin is an organ no different from the heart or kidneys or any of the other organs. The body is a massive coming together of different elements of the earth that, when brought together and "enlivened", make up what most of us consider the total "person."

To put this another way: the body is like a walking/talking conglomeration of the earth. As it is stated at many funerals: "ashes to ashes, and dust to dust." Most adults know that their bodies at death disintegrate and go back into the earth. So your body is the aspect of you that can "identify" with the solid aspect of nature itself.

Nature has a physical aspect, a gross aspect, and it is this aspect that you experience through your senses. It is interesting to note that almost all faiths agree that people are given approximately 70 years to live. Therefore people are in fact given 70 years to "identify" and have "experience" of this gross physical Earth aspect of creation.

On some level, you may understand that your body is actually a manifestation of the earth, but you do not "know" it. Many people think that their body is the sum total of who they are. The body is considered to be the lower aspect of a person as it is from the earth, which is lower than the heavens.

The Soul

There is nothing in creation that is not at its base a Soul. Some may call this Soul God. Some call it energy. Some may even call it consciousness. Whatever you may want to call it, every living thing has it. We know this is so, because it is the absence of this "soul stuff" that constitutes death. When this "soul stuff" leaves the body, that person is said to have died. When this "soul stuff" leaves an animal, it is said that the animal has died. It is this "Soul" which enlivens the gross elements of creation (the body) and gives what we call life to the natural world. This soul differs from the body because it exists on all planes of consciousness simultaneously, whereas the body exists only in time and space. (A.k.a. as Earth)

Additionally, it is this spiritual aspect of you that has the exact same nature of the Divine. An analogy may be helpful here. Soul is similar to you standing on the beach in California with your feet in the Pacific Ocean. If you took a cup and put one drop of water from the Pacific Ocean in the cup, would the water drop in the cup's constituency change from that of the Pacific Ocean itself? Would the appearance of the separation of the water droplet from the rest of the ocean water change its consistency from that of the whole? In essence, would the water drop all of a sudden stop being Pacific Ocean water? Of course not.

The only thing that changes in this example is the location of the water droplet. It always remains Pacific Ocean water. Even if it "forgot" that it was in fact Pacific Ocean water, that doesn't change what it is. As soon it is placed back in the ocean, it becomes one with the entire ocean once more. That is exactly how the soul of a person is. The soul of a person is the water droplet in the cup which appears to be separated from the rest of the ocean. The Pacific Ocean is Spirit.

The soul's consistency is no different from the overall Spirit, or the ocean from the example. It just appears to be separated from the whole by being separated by a body instead of a cup. As beings, the cup housing the soul is your own body. The soul is the higher aspect of a person. It is the

51

same as the Spirit but just in a much smaller degree.

Now this part is key. Since it is this Spirit which gives that which we call life, and since we agree that this Spirit/energy/stuff/consciousness is eternal, then if any aspect of our being is real, it would have to be this part.

The Mind/Senses

These two aspects work together to provide balance so you can operate equally between the lower physical realm (the body) and the higher spiritual realm (the soul).

Your senses are designed to experience the lower realm. Everything you can see, feel, taste, touch, and hear is all in the physical realm. The mind—in fact a purified mind—is needed for you to experience the spiritual aspect of your being.

So the mind/senses allow you to simultaneously experience both the higher and lower realms of existence—but only when fed properly and used properly. Any unbalanced focus on one over the other, leads to a host of problems. An unbalanced focus occurs when one reinforces the **idea** that they are exclusively the "body" only, or that they are exclusively the "spirit" only.

So now you have it. These are the three aspects of a being which together make up the 'whole of you'. Body, mind/senses, and soul therefore have to be nurtured and fed. It is these three that grow and mature and evolve through the consumption of a healthy diet. And it is these three aspects that when fed properly and balanced, help prepare you to "experience" the higher aspect of your being. The nature of spirit.

FOOD FOR THE BODY

The popular diet of people in the United States and in the western-influenced world is a diet composed primarily of meats and processed foods. It has been this way for approximately 100 years. Prior to that time, much of the food consumed was a vegetable and fruit diet. Granted meat was a part of many meals, it was not as prevalent then and eaten in the degree to which it is today.

During this time many people ate the food which they had on their land. As a vegetable and fruit diet could be grown regularly and in large quantities, they were our staples. Conversely, because many people only had on their farms animals that needed time to grow and give birth to other animals, it is not surprising that the eating of meat happened far less during this time.

It was not until the late 1800s and early 1900s that the cattleman became 'the meat industry' as mass production meant organized methods of breeding and birthing, and a rapid rate rise in the growth process of animals. More and more people could eat meat more often. This coincided with the development of processed foods. In a way the processing of food was necessary for the food industry. Anyone who has ever purchased an organic food (a food grown with no chemical additives or preservatives), or someone who has grown food in their own garden, has noticed that the food spoils much faster than foods that have been treated with preservatives.

Since the turn of the last century a host of foods eaten by the majority of people have contained a lot of preservatives to keep that food on the shelves longer. It could be argued that preserving the longevity of a food is a good thing. But what about the side effects associated with the consumption of preservatives in the food?

Preservatives have an effect on the body and it's not a good one. The research is there for those who want to see it. Visit your local library to read books and articles that explain in detail just what we do to our bodies by eating foods that contain preservatives.

I do not intend to discuss the medical evidence associated with a preservative-laden diet. What will be stated is this: preservatives are chemicals that are not natural to the body. They are in fact foreign substances and are not from the earth. They are chemicals no different from the chemicals that make up alcohol, cigarettes, cocaine, or other drugs. What do foreign chemicals and substances do in the body? We know that alcohol, cocaine, and other drugs give one a false sense of reality. They skew your perception of what is real and what is not. Is there any reason to believe that the preservatives and chemicals in food do not also skew your perception of reality as well? Just because everyone appears to be the same does not mean that everyone's perception is not skewed. Consider this: No one recognizes that their perception is skewed because everyone else's perception is the same.

So chemicals in foods are not good for the body. In fact since this country has been consuming such a processed food diet, the rate of degenerative disease, (cancer, diabetes etc.,) has grown to an outlandish degree. Prior to the advent of a meat, preservative and chemical-laden diet, cancer, diabetes and other degenerative diseases occurred rarely if at all.

Now about meat. Meat is very difficult to digest. According to the Federal Drug Administration (FDA), every person in the United States is currently walking around with between 10-40 pounds of undigested meat in their system.

Undigested meat putrefies, and becomes toxic. Toxic things turn into poisons in the body. These poisons over time often cause cancer. Additionally, animals are given growth hormones to stimulate their development. The faster an animal grows, the faster it can be killed and sold. The body development of children at younger and younger ages and the problems of obesity should not be surprising given the hormones injected into animals to speed their growth. The evidence is compelling that meat is an unnatural substance for the body, not good for it in any way.

Manmade chemicals, and preservatives and meat are simply not proper fuel for the body. They actually cause a state of being which moves a person further away from being able to perceive reality as it is. The next time you see someone on television who has committed some type of terrible crime and they are referred to as an animal, just remember "you are what you eat."

FOOD FOR THE MIND & SENSES

The mind and senses need to be fed just like the body. The **idea** that mind/senses do not require proper nutrition is mistaken. Often people do not realize that the mind/sense complex needs proper fuel. So, people do not pay attention to the importance of feeding this aspect of their being. However, the inability to recognize the need to feed the mind/senses does not mean that it is not being fed.

Proper food for your mind is important because it helps you to have the life you claim you want. A life in which you are happy at all times no matter what is going on around you. A life that is peaceful and contented. A life that is free from worry and anxiety even if things are happening that could be considered to be negative. People are not aware that the mind/sense's *idea of reality* is created through the food that it consumes. People feed this aspect of their being unconsciously. People are often oblivious to the fact that their *idea of reality* is shaped by stimuli over which they exercise no control.

Everything that you interact with through your sense of sight and of sound is food for the mind. Therefore every article or book that you read is food for the mind. Every movie or television show that you see is food for the mind. Every song or music that you hear is food for the mind.

The mind is no different from the body—it, too, needs nutritious food to function at its optimal level. Have you ever looked consciously and critically at what you allow to enter into your mental space, your mind? Is it good for you? Do the images that come into your mind help you become more peaceful, contented and happy? Or do they create ideas and images that lead to frustration, strife, worry and anxiety? Look at what you consume every day and you will see the answer.

Conversations with co-workers can be filled with talk about parts of the job that people dislike—from duties to the boss or other co-workers. Many of our popular movies and television programs contain very graphic violence and sex. Daily newspapers and news shows headline those deeds that are heinous in nature. Very violent acts. Acts that involve stealing. Acts that involve war. So much of our music is no different. The same images: violence and sex.

How much thought do you give to what effect all this 'sensory food' has on your mind/senses and how this food shapes your **idea of reality**? Do you see the effect that these foods have on your ability to have the life that you want? A life that is filled with happiness. A life filled with joy. A life filled with peace and contentment. For most of us, the constant bombardment of the mind with negative sights and sounds doesn't make us all become violent. Indeed, most of us are not affected in this way, but the effect on us is just as bad. All of these negative images in the mind create a feeling of uneasiness. It creates an internal form of anxiety. It also creates an internal form of worry. Unfortunately the feelings are internal and subtle. It takes a significant amount of reflection to recognize the subtle aspects of your being. Most of us do not reflect on these types of matters; therefore many of us don't recognize that they exist.

It is true that you are what you eat. This applies to what you eat for your mind as well. A look at the "mind-set" of western society shows pretty clearly what types of foods some people are consuming for their minds. Society as a whole is very violent. For those of us who are not violent, most of us tolerate violence. Much of society seems to lack morals and integrity. Many people talk morality but do not LIVE it. Many talk about integrity but compromise themselves on a regular basis. For those who do not lack morals and integrity, immoral behavior is tolerated.

We focus on and fight over our differences instead of coming together around what we share. There are people who stand in the synagogues, churches, mosques and other places of God, and teach that the only way to peace is through war. Peace through killing. For them, somehow God justifies the killing of others.

I believe that this reflects the diet of so many—a diet for the mind that is poisonous and toxic. Although you cannot get cancer of the mind, your mind can still become diseased. Anyone who justifies killing for ANY reason—while talking about how religious they are—has a disease-laden mind. People that make excuses for those who have done terrible acts to children because they have been involved in the church for a long time, have a disease-laden mind. Those that justify discrimination, slavery, and a host of other oppressive acts while professing a belief in whatever religious or moral doctrine they have, are people with a disease-laden mind.

A simple look at society shows the type of food for the mind that people have available and are eating. Again, you are what you eat.

FOOD FOR THE SOUL

The spirit/soul/energy/consciousness—whatever you want to call it— also needs to be fed a proper and nutritious diet. In this society, people feed this aspect of themselves by going to a temple, a synagogue, a church, a mosque or whatever their particular religious gathering place is called.

People go to feed their Soul. But participating in religious gatherings does not actually feed their soul. They are feeding their mind while thinking they are feeding their soul.

As stated previously, the spirit/soul/energy/consciousness of a person is that aspect that exists at all times simultaneously on all planes of existence. It is that aspect that gives what is called "life" to the conglomeration of matter known as a body. Once the soul leaves the body, then what is known as death occurs. However death has really not occurred. The body was only 'enlivened' by the soul. The body never really was "alive".

Once the soul leaves the body, the soul still exists. Soul does not and cannot die. It is, has been, and always shall be. This is important to realize in reflecting upon proper food for the spiritual aspect of the being.

Soul is not the body. It IS what people call life of the body. So feeding of the soul cannot occur through the body. You must **"identify"** with the spiritual aspect of your self to feed it that which is proper and nutritious for it. To identify with the "soul" one must have a purified mind.

As stated previously, the senses allow one to identify with the gross conglomeration of earth elements. The senses allow one to be aware of all that exists in this realm. However, the senses give one a skewed view of reality. Our eyes can only see so far. If we could see like a telescope sees, our **idea** of reality would be different. If we could hear and smell like a dog, our **idea** of reality would be different. So the senses cannot be used to **"identify"** with the soul because the soul transcends all that is.

This is why the modern approach to feeding the soul (attending a temple, synagogue, church or mosque) does not feed the soul. This attendance and worship in fact feeds the mind as these actions are experienced through the senses.

To feed the soul, you must transcend the senses. Transcendence of the senses occurs through meditation once you have obtained a purified mind. Meditation is practicing mental exercises that enable you, over time, to stop the vibrations of the mind due to unwanted thoughts. I recommend that you read "Meditation" by Dr. Muata Ashby to explore the process of meditation.

Once your mind is stilled through meditation, you can then "experience" that aspect of yourself that is expansive and complete without limits. This aspect is your soul. It is this "experience" that actually feeds your soul. People have forgotten that they are in actuality a soul having a human experience. The more you feed your soul, the more you experience your higher nature, and the more you become one with yourself.

This is proper food for the soul. Food that lets your soul "remember" that it is a soul and not a body.

Notice that this "experience" is not experienced through the senses. It occurs beyond them. There is no use for taste, touch, hearing, sight and smelling while in the meditative state. These senses are transcended.

You do need a purified mind so that meditation will work as effectively as it can. A purified mind is a mind that is not controlled by its thoughts and desires. A purified mind does not allow you to get upset or angry when things do not go your way. A purified mind does not allow you to get sullen or depressed because of life's changing tendencies. A purified mind is a mind that does not allow you to cause yourself frustration.

All of these emotions and feelings keep your mind "moving" as it were. Moving from one thought to the next. Moving from one emotion to the next based upon the next thought. All thoughts and desires keep the mind "moving". A "moving" mind is an agitated mind. A "still" mind is needed to experience that aspect of yourself that is expansive and without limits. A "still" mind for purposes of this chapter only is a purified mind.

How do you get a purified mind that will allow meditation to be effective? By consuming a mental diet based on all of the things that people say they want. Peace. Joy. Love. Happiness.

For every two hours that you watch a violent movie, replace that with viewing something which involves those beautiful attributes you want. Pay attention to how much time you engage in activity or behavior that consciously or unconsciously involves those things you want to escape. There is only certain programming on television or at the movies that should be viewed. There are only certain types of music that should be listened to.

There are only certain types of books and articles that should be read.

Do you really want peace, joy, contentment, and happiness? If so, then begin feeding yourself with the types of materials that will subconsciously and unconsciously begin moving you in this direction. This is how you purify your mind. By providing it with only those things that promote what you want out of life. Once the process to purify your mind has begun, then you are in the position to begin feeding the soul. The actual feeding of the soul occurs through meditation. As you become more and more aware of the aspect of yourself that is expansive and unlimited through the meditation process, you gradually stop believing that you are your body only. As you experience this aspect of yourself more and more, you begin to "remember" this aspect of yourself more and more.

It is as if this memory had been forgotten. Forgotten because you grew to believe the **idea** that you are only the body. Feeding of the soul is you "remembering" yourself as expansive and unlimited. The more you feed yourself (the more you "remember") the more you are able to have that which you say you want out of life. Happiness, joy, peace, and so on.

YOU are expansive.

YOU are unlimited.

Once you fully and totally "remember" this aspect of yourself, you will experience COMPLETE FULFILLMENT.

FOOD FOR THE BODY, MIND & SPIRIT

You are much more than a body that is given approximately 70 years to live. However this is the **idea** that perpetuates society. Every person is born with the ability to recognize the depths of their being right now. Do YOU have an **idea about life** which allows the recognition of the depths of your being right now?

Whose **idea** was it that said that you must die before you can discover the essence of life? No one has come back from the dead that I am aware of, so how do we know this **idea** is true? If death is needed for ultimate understanding then **what's the point of life?** If this **idea** of death before understanding life is not true, then you could find yourself living an entire lifetime under an **illusion**—an **illusion** that may keep you from discovering the depths of your existence today and in this lifetime. Is this an **idea** that YOU consciously chose? Is this **idea** actually a true **idea** or is it now a mistaken **idea** that has simply become **reality** for you?

A diet that is nutritious on ALL levels is necessary when you are seeking the answer to the central question of life "Who Am I". A nutritious diet on all levels is needed to take control over all the aspects of your life. It is also the foundation needed so that you can achieve COMPLETE FULFILLMENT before you die.

Are you only a body? Is the **idea** that you are the body and only the body, is that **idea** one that will stand the test of time? If your **idea** of who you are is more than this body, do you act in accordance with your **idea?**

If the answer to any of these questions is "no", do you manifest YOUR idea? Do you "see" yourself as the Mind, Body, and Soul conglomeration, or do you "see" yourself as one or two parts only?

The **idea** perpetuated about nutrition for the body fails to account for two significant aspects of a person: the mind/senses and the soul. Is this an **idea** that you unconsciously believe to be true?

Unconscious or ingrained beliefs that are based on *mistaken* **ideas** are illusions which will not stand the test of time!

REFLECTION:

1   What is YOUR *Idea* about what constitutes malnutrition?
2   Will this *Idea* change now that YOU have read this chapter?
3   Will YOUR new *Idea* about Nutrition have a better chance at standing the test of time?

CHAPTER 5

I May Forgive You, But I Will Never Forget!
(Forgiveness)

REFLECTION:

1   The Forgive-but-not-Forget *Idea* about forgiveness is common. Are there any other *Ideas* about Forgiveness?
2   Do YOU utilize the Forgive-but-not-Forget *Idea*?
3   If yes, where did YOU get the *Idea* from?
4   Was it a conscious choice or was it something YOU adopted based on what everyone else does?

The **idea** to forgive but not forget has been around for quite awhile. Is there anyone that has not accepted this **idea** about forgiveness as they deal with unpleasant circumstances in their life? What is gained by the acceptance of this **idea**? Most importantly what is lost? These issues and more will be addressed in this chapter.

Most of us have used the phrase "I may forgive but I will never forget." The failure to forgive COMPLETELY is one of the most difficult obstacles to your living a spiritual life. The statement *I will forgive but I will never forget* makes it clear to us why it is an obstacle. If you can't forget, then you can't forgive.

We often think that time will heal all wounds. We also think that getting away from the person for, or from, whom forgiveness may be needed, will help the situation. These thoughts on forgiveness do not go deep enough in understanding the process required to completely forgive another. This is only a surface forgiveness—something that happens outside of yourself. It is like the frosting on a cake.

Unfortunately with this surface mindset, it can take a traumatic event to get you to realize just how tightly you've been holding onto animosity, judgment, resentment, and a host of other negative thoughts. To completely

61

forgive someone, you need to have a thorough understanding of the nature of hurt or pain. People do not COMPLETELY forgive because they have not stopped COMPLETELY hurting. In fact in many instances, years could go by after a hurtful event, but the pain from that event is no different in the future than it was when you were originally hurt. As we explore forgiveness in this section, we will also analyze the nature of hurt or pain and how it works in the human psyche. Understanding the whole process will help you analyze if forgiving without forgetting works. In other words, is the **idea** of forgiving without forgetting true?

To live a spiritual life you have to learn to let go of attachments to **ideas** and things which are not true. Things that are not based in reality: the thought that someone has hurt you is an **idea** that is not true. All forgiveness is based on the premise that you have been wronged or hurt. In reality you have not been hurt. You just believe that you have been. Your personality or ego is what is hurt. However, YOU are not the personality. YOU are not the ego. YOU are much more than this. YOU (the Real You) cannot be hurt.

ALTHOUGH A CLOUD MAY BLOCK THE VIEW OF THE SUN, THE SUN IS ALWAYS SHINING

The inability to completely forgive, (the **idea** that you have been hurt by another) acts in you like a cloud does to the sun when it is front of it. It blocks your ability to see beyond what appears to be real to the personality or ego. Just like you may think that the sun has not come out when blocked by the clouds, if you have not completely forgiven, then you are holding onto a false **idea**. And it is that false **idea** that keeps you tied to the belief that you have been hurt or wronged. In reality, YOU (the real you) cannot be hurt or traumatized. The real YOU is like the sun that is always shining. It is only that aspect of your being that is not real, your personality/ego that can be hurt.

The personality/ego of a person is very similar to that of a cloud. You cannot hold onto the personality. It does not have a substance. However, over long periods of time, the personality/ego clouds your ability to see the actual aspect of yourself. You then forget the reality. Your inability to

62

completely forgive acts in you like a cloud in front of the sun.

THE "IDEA" OF BEING HURT

To forgive completely, you must first understand the different emotional and psychological layers that have built in a person hurt by another. As stated previously, hurt itself, or the **idea** of being hurt, is the root of the problem.

People often grow up believing that there is a certain way that their life should unfold—a certain way their lives should happen. People think that their life is supposed to be a bed of roses. This idea of how you believe your life should be is a *"make-believe reality."* It is *make-believe* because rarely is your life a reflection of how you believe it should be. As a result, it is easy for a subtle form of discontent and/or sadness to form deep within your subconscious. A feeling that consciously is not realized. It is this "feeling" that is described as "hurt." The feeling that your life is not good because it is not the way you believe it should be.

The contradiction between the *"make believe reality,"* and the *"actual reality"* creates the feelings described as hurt or pain. Often it is not the actual circumstance that creates the "hurt." It is the **idea** of how things should be differing from the actual reality that causes the "hurt."

I FORGIVE YOU,
BUT WILL NEVER FORGET WHAT YOU
DID TO ME!

Now let's look at the term "I will forgive but I will never forget." Do you know this to be true? I mean have you ever forgiven someone but chose not to forget what they had done to you? Have you ever thought or wondered why you won't forget? Some of us make the choice of not forgetting to insure that it doesn't happen again. If you reflect on making the decision to not forget, you will typically find that you are not normally around the person you are upset with. The other person is in most instances completely out the picture of your life. If your dad walked out on you when you were younger and you now choose to not forget this fact, recognize that in all likelihood your dad is no longer a part of your life. In this case you do not see your father on a daily or regular basis. He may even live in an entirely different city or state.

If you had a spouse who did not treat you in a manner that you felt was appropriate, by the time you get to the *I forgive but will not forgive* state, the relationship is over, and one of you has moved out. If one of you has not moved out physically, someone has moved out emotionally. What is the point of not forgetting what someone did to you, to hurt you, if they are no longer around you? Can a person who is no longer in your life hurt you anymore? A person no longer a part of your life cannot hurt you in the same way that they did when you were together. If you reflect on it, having the-forgive-but-not-forget mindset once a person is no longer a part of your life is not necessary. In fact it may even be harmful to your personally. Harmful because it acts like a cloud—a veil—and reinforces the "make believe reality" created by a person.

For those people who remain in a relationship with someone that has hurt them, you may be saying, well I need to stay on top of the situation so that I don't act foolishly again. I have to watch this person and myself to make sure I don't wind up in the same situation again. Keep in mind the following: staying in the midst of a situation and forcing you to constantly "protect" yourself from another person by "not forgetting" the way they are creates a victim mentality mindset. The decision to not forget reinforces the **idea** that you were victimized by the other person.

So choosing to forgive but not forget, in any circumstance, is choosing to be a victim of the circumstance instead of choosing to conquer it.

This does not mean that you should keep yourself around another who is harmful to you physically or emotionally. It is in your own best interest to get yourself out from the situation entirely. However physically removing yourself is only half the battle. Emotionally removing yourself is the other half, and as long as you choose to never forget, then you are in fact mentally still choosing to be a victim of the situation.

THE NATURE OF THE HUMAN BEING
(Ego/Personality)

Why is it is difficult to forget? Because forgiveness has only happened on the outside.

Before going any further, the nature of the entity we call the "human being" needs to be understood. This understanding is important for you to achieve complete forgiveness. The human being is a collection of physical elements (matter) lumped together and infused with what some call 'energy, soul, or spirit', or what some others call 'consciousnesses. Whatever you want to name it, this is how we are all put together. But there is another aspect to our collection that is not made up of anything and not visible. Yet it's just as real to you as your physical bodies and "energy." This aspect is your **ego**, or **personality**.

You cannot touch your ego/personality like you can your body. You cannot conduct scientific experiments to discover the ego/personality in the same way that you can with energy. The ego/personality is not real in that sense. In real terms the ego/personality is an **idea** about who you are. And like many other **ideas**, it is simply an illusion.

We don't recognize that the ego is not real. That it is illusory. We believe it to be real and so we act in accordance with that belief. But it is self-created, and we created our ego/personality based upon our life circumstances. Our environment. Our culture.

Through societal ritual—how people act and react—you have learned to believe that happiness has a certain look that you recognize as 'happiness', or that 'sad' has another look, or that 'fun' looks a particular way, and so on. These environmental **ideas** form the basis of your personality, and because none of us knows any better, we never recognize that all of these **ideas** about emotions and how they appear are simply just that, **ideas** that constitute a "make believe reality." The **ideas** are not real in and of themselves. People adopt these **ideas** as their own and over time believe them to be true. Hence the personality of the person is created. This forms the basic personality structure.

In the same way that our personality is formed by how others act and react, so too is many of our **ideas** about what is good and bad in others, and in us. If others treat a person in a particular way because of the color of their skin or the shape of their eyes that *"make believe reality"* becomes what we 'know' to be true; it is another **idea** that will not stand the test of time.

The foundation that you must understand in the context of complete forgiveness is recognizing that your personality/ego is not real. It is an illusion about 'who' you are that you have created. This is the key. From this understanding you will gain a better appreciation for how you build layers on your 'personality' from this mistaken **idea**.

LAYERS OF THE PERSONALITY

You develop layers of your personality as you grow and identify with environmental stimuli which you accept as real. Layers form on top of the initial first belief (identification). In time this belief becomes real as people identify with it. The overall personality develops based upon different categories of the environmental stimuli. Categories include but are not limited to what constitutes sadness, pain, joy, love and a host of others. Let's examine happiness for a moment.

If one believes from their early childhood that happiness is found in the acquisition of objects, (identification) then over time you will develop an affinity for certain types of objects to bring about your happiness.

- This affinity forms the first layer: the belief that this particular type of object will make you happy. As soon as this layer is established, immediately and simultaneously a second layer is developed.

- This next layer is the belief that if you do not have this type or types of objects, you will be unhappy. This layer happens unconsciously and many if not most people do not realize that this layer even exists.

- A third layer is simultaneously created when this second layer comes into existence. The third layer manifests as upset-ness over not being able to acquire the particular object that you have developed the affinity for.

- The final layer develops when you act out on your upset-ness and begin blaming others (people, life, God) for your inability to have the objects that you have believed will make you happy. This layering process occurs in many areas of your life.

Your beliefs about life and how it is to be lived is "learned behavior" that has been practiced over time. It is taught through your environment. Through these lessons, different layers of your personality are developed.

Now what do these layers have to do with complete forgiveness? Everything. It is the failure to understand the different layers of the personality which prevents people from being able to completely forgive. It is the inability to understand the *"make believe reality"*. It is this inability which keeps one always in the state in which one will never "forget." This plays itself out most often in opposite sex relationships of husband/wife or boyfriend/girlfriend. It also occurs in relationships between parents and children. I know this to be true because as this piece is being written, I am dealing with my inability to completely forgive in both circumstances.

I had once thought that I had learned how to master the art of complete forgiveness. I was wrong. I was wrong because I had not yet fully understood the different layers of the personality. Because of this inability, I missed out on something that I really wanted.

Let me share this with you. At the time of this writing, it was two weeks to the day that my father made his transition. He died of a stroke on March 23, 2006. He was not sick, nor had he complained of feeling unwell. From what I have been told there was nothing unusual about his health. One Wednesday evening he had a stroke, went into a coma, and the following day he died. He was 64.

Now my relationship with my father was not great. In fact I would say that it was darn right awful. My dad did not spend much time with me or my two brothers and sister. As a result, I grew up disliking him a great deal. As a child, I held out hope that he would love me and that we could have what I thought was the father-son relationship. As I became a teenager and a young man in my late teens and early twenties, my hope changed to anger and resentment. As I grew into my thirties, the anger subsided and at one point in my mind, I let him go. I "forgave" him for not being there for me. But I just could not and would not <u>forget</u> what he had done to me. He deprived me of having a father.

That was something that I just could not forget. In the summer of 2005, he came to Detroit and spent about three weeks visiting his family. He lived in Memphis, Tennessee at the time but most of his siblings live in Detroit. I saw him once during that time but I admit I was not enthusiastic about seeing him. I was short with him and kept our conversation to a minimum. I had not "forgotten" what he did to me all those years ago, so really there was not much for me to say to him. Well, I guess he must have known his time was limited, because that was the last time me and the rest of the family in Detroit saw him alive.

Once my father died, of course everything changed. There was no longer anything left for me to make sure I didn't <u>forget</u>. He was gone and was not coming back.

Why was it so difficult for me to forget how he had been with me? Because I did not understand the layering process of my personality. I did not understand that as a young boy, I developed the first layer. An **idea**, a *"make believe reality"* about how a father was supposed to be with his son. I did not understand that as this **idea** developed, at the same time I unconsciously created the second layer: The means by which I would think that I was unhappy.

Namely, as soon as the **idea** of what a father was supposed to do or be was not there in my life, then I would immediately be unhappy.

I did not understand that as I grew into my teen age and young adult years, the next layer would develop out of that same unhappiness. That layer was made of resentment, frustration and anger. So I created for myself a situation which frankly would not allow me to "forget."

I had now become a victim. 'Poor me' who did not get the type of relationship I thought of. I had an **idea** according to my *"make believe idea"* about what a father-son relationship looked like. How could I ever "forget" this wrong done to me? I couldn't. At least I thought I couldn't. And I did not. And this inability hurt me. Not him.

Because of this mindset, I was not able to see things about my father that were right there in front of me. I could not see that my father like all people had his own set of issues. That he was doing the best he knew how to do. That if he could have done better he would have. That in his own way, he cared about me a great deal. It may not have looked like I wanted it to, but he did nevertheless. That without him, I would not be on this planet. And that in spite of everything, I still turned out okay. Had this cloud (this mindset) not been in front of me, I would have been different with my father when he visited that summer of 2005. He then would have been different with me. Had this cloud (mindset) not been in front of me, my relationship with him over the years would have been different as well.

Ultimately, complete forgiveness can only happen when you realize that the foundation of the hurt has occurred in the realm of your personality/ego. It is the ego that believes it has been hurt based upon **IDEAS** you create in your "*make believe reality*."

I thought that I should have had a particular type of father. I didn't, so my personality/ego was hurt. Had I grown up thinking that the world did not promise me a rose garden, my **idea** about how my father should have been would have been different. I would have had nothing to "forget" because my **IDEA** of what I was not getting would have been different. I then would not have been a victim of anything because I would not have seen myself as being wronged.

- YOU have not been wronged.
- YOU have not been hurt.
- YOU do not have anyone to forgive.
- YOUR self-created *make believe reality* is that which has been hurt…it is a 'reality' that is, in fact, an *illusion*.

Let go of this/these false **ideas** on forgiveness. Ultimately they turn you into a person with a victim mentality. Victims cannot be strong people. You can act tough on the outside, but if you carry with you the 'victim hood', you are weak on the inside. Think positive as much as you want, but the underlying **idea** of being a victim automatically cancels out the positive thinking. In fact, it negates your power.

If you choose to never forget, you give away a very important aspect of yourself: the ability to believe, deep inside your very soul, how **GREAT**

YOU ARE! Victims are not great. Victims are weak. Television, movies—even the dictionaries—all confirm how low and weak the rest of the world places victims. The **idea** to "not forget" is the **idea** to be <u>a victim</u>.

The victim **idea** sabotages your willpower to accomplish what you desire. Simply put, you will not be all that you can be if you hold onto a sense of 'victimhood'.

Is the present **idea** in society about forgiveness true? Does this **idea** foster the type of you that YOU consciously desire? Are you a victim of anything? Or did you at some point create a *"make believe reality"* that just didn't happen according to your thoughts?

REFLECTION:

1   Does the forgive-but-not-forget *Idea* create a victim mentality?
2   What are YOUR thoughts on the *"make believe reality"* in this chapter?
3   What is YOUR present *Idea* on Forgiveness?
4   Are there any others?
5   From today forward, which *Idea* will YOU choose?

"Do Not Allow What You Think,
Or The Way You Think To
<u>*Limit*</u>
What You Think,
Or The Way You Think!"

-By: Anpu Waset

SECTION II

WAYS OF BEING

Ways of Being are *"practices"* that initially enforce and, over time, reinforce the so called reality of a previously chosen mistaken **idea**. These *"practices"* create a mindset that becomes rigid and inflexible to the possibility that the original **idea** was not true.

Remember the passage in Obstacles about the world being flat? This, of course, was an untrue **idea**.

"Practices" that enforced the flat-earth **idea** were:
- maps drawn up showing everyone—sailors, merchants, military leaders—a flat world.
- everything taught—science, history, mathematics—based on 'the truth' that the world was flat.
- no one sailed beyond different parts of the world.

Everyone assumed that the world was nothing other than flat. Assuming itself is a *"practice"* because it requires a conscious thought. Thinking is an active process even though we don't look at it that way. When you think, you are in fact "doing" something. Thinking thoughts in harmony with an untrue **idea**—such as "the world is flat so I know I will fall off the edge if I sail too far—is also a *"practice."*

The chapters in this section are *"practices"* common to many of us that reinforce previously accepted untrue **ideas**. These *"practices"* enforce the belief that the untrue **idea** is **REAL**!

CHAPTER 6

PRACTICE MAKES PERFECT

REFLECTION:

1   **Does Practice make Perfect?**
2   **What do YOU regularly Practice?**
3   **Do these Practices help YOU answer the question *Who Am I*?**
4   **Do these Practices help YOU take charge and control of Your life?**

You've heard the term practice makes perfect? Do you think that there is truth to the statement? If practice does eventually make one perfect, what is it that people generally practice? If this is true, how does what one practices relate to one's ability to live a spiritual life? This chapter will address this issue.

Many people don't see obstacles that affect their ability to live a spiritual life. Often these are not realized because people are accustomed to doing them on a regular basis. This chapter was written to bring attention to the everyday "things" that people "practice" that reinforce *mistaken* **ideas** that they believe is real. You can get so caught up in "living life" that you don't realize the impact that this way of living is having on you. These "practices" are a form of living life on automatic pilot.

An actual pilot watches the plane and is there in case something goes wrong, but the plane actually flies itself through the computer. Many people's entire way of living life is by way of their own automatic pilot. Just think about it: people do the same things over and over again without a thought.

These activities are "practices" as they are done over and over again. It is no wonder that after 10, 15, 20 and more years of living like this, people wonder where their life went. It is this everyday unconscious living that will be analyzed in the context of its effect on your ability to live a spiritual life.

Before we go too far into this topic, let's look at whether the phrase itself "practice makes perfect" has any merit.

Does practice actually make one perfect? Does it make one better than they were before? If so, how does this apply to living a spiritual life? How does this apply to living based upon a *mistaken* **idea**? What are some of the things that people practice? Do they get better at those things? Does this practice make the person a better person? Specifically does the practice help a person become more peaceful and contented? Or does it make one bitter or frustrated?

Does Practice Make You Perfect?

Conscious Practice vs. Unconscious Practice

Does the name Tiger Woods ring a bell? In case you missed the sports news over the past few years, Tiger is the number one golfer in the world. Everyone agrees that he is simply the best golfer in the world. Do you think that he became the number one player in the world without practicing the game?

I read somewhere a few years ago that in his younger days he played golf twelve to sixteen hours a day. I also read that for him, a lot of this time he did not consider as "practice". He considered it fun because golf is what he enjoys doing. Now even though he did not consider playing the game that much as practice, he did spend quite a bit of time working on different aspects of his game. The devoted time to practice his golf game was a CONSCIOUS choice that he made to become a better golfer. He chose to practice to improve.

A funny thing happened to him though. About three years after becoming the number one player in the world, he decided to change his golf swing. Now remember, he was the number one player in the world already. Changing a golf swing in the sport of golf is equivalent to changing from writing with your right hand to writing with your left hand. Everyone thought he was crazy, and for about two years, he began losing tournaments that he had previously been winning. People started to say that his time of being 'the best' was over. Tiger Woods CONSCIOUSLY changed his golf swing and practiced the new swing for about two years before it became natural for him. It didn't take him long to resume his number one world ranking as he started to win once more.

Do you think that in the case of Mr. Woods that practice made him perfect? I don't know if he would say he is the perfect golfer, but practice has definitely made him the number one golfer, i.e. the best golfer in the world.

This is one example of where it appears that a conscious choice to "practice" does in fact make one perfect. Or at least it makes one very good. At least in the case of Tiger Woods, it made him the best at what he does. Now this is an example of a conscious choice to practice something to get better at it.

Now let's look at examples of UNCONSCIOUS practices that make you perfect or at least much better than you were before.

Let's look at the example of driving a car. Why is a 16-year-old person not considered to be a good driver? Because they haven't driven that long. They haven't had much "practice." This is why insurance rates for young people are expensive.

It can be argued that older drivers are better drivers because they have more experience. They have had more "practice" driving. Now reflect on the following: Does the fact that someone is driving over a longer period of time make them "REALIZE" that they are in fact getting more "practice" at driving? When a person gets behind the wheel of that car, are they getting in the car to "practice" their driving? No. They get in the car to go to work. They get in the car to go to a party. They get in the car to go to the store. They don't get into it to "practice" driving. But the more they drive, the more "practice" they get. This unconscious "practice" of driving over time makes one perfect, or at least a better driver. Do you agree?

So now we've talked about two different examples of 'practicing' situations. The first involved an example in which a person made a conscious choice to "practice" something to become better at it (Tiger Woods and golf.) The second example involved a situation in which a person became better at doing something (driving) that they unconsciously "practiced" over an extended period of time.

So by now you can see that the conscious and unconscious practice of something will make one perfect, or at a minimum will make them much better at it. Now with that done as a foundation, let's discuss some of the unconscious ways of being that people practice that unbeknown to them they have become proficient at.

What Do People Unconsciously Practice?

This chapter is one of my favorites because it hit so close to home for me in many ways. You see there are many things that people do on a regular basis that they do not think about. Anything a person does on a regular basis, that person is in fact "practicing" that behavior, that thing. Whether it is driving their car or ironing a shirt, doing something regularly is "practicing" that thing. It is of course an unconscious "practice," but it is a "practice" nevertheless.

It has been my experience in my more than 43 years on this planet that people unconsciously "practice" the following on a regular basis. Being frustrated. Being angry. Being disappointed. Being upset. Being a liar. Being deceitful. Being sullen. Being one who gossips. Being resentful. Being impatient. Being one who likes to argue. Being jealous. Being envious. Being one who thinks ill about others. Being one who is prideful based upon their possessions.

These are the things I see people "practice" on a daily basis. They are unconscious "practices" but "practices" nevertheless. These "practices" are considered and accepted as normal.

Let me give you an example. If you are driving down the road and someone cuts you off, the response for many of us is to get upset and even downright angry. In some parts of the country people actually shoot at other people in road rage incidents.

We don't stop to think about our reaction. Worse yet, we continue doing this over and over again. Any repetitive and continuous cycle is a "practice." So guess what happens? You become better and better at becoming angry when someone cuts you off. And conversely, it becomes harder and harder for you to become peaceful and contented. That's why people don't really mellow with age.

Many who we think have 'mellowed out' have actually 'tuckered out'. They have drained so much of the energy from themselves that they are simply tired. However, many people stay irritated throughout their entire lives.

We've all heard the phrase *a leopard can't change its spots*. I don't believe that it is true. These spots can be changed. However, it can only be done one way—by "practicing" something else.

I submit to you that there are many areas in people's lives where they unconsciously engage in "practices" that lead them towards a great deal of pain and anguish. The exact opposite of what they want—happiness, peace and contentment. The more they "practice," the better they become at it and the harder it becomes for them to get out of that way of being. They become skilled at making their own lives miserable.

"Practice" does make one perfect—even if it is in ways that make us miserable.

By now you may be asking, what does any of this have to do with living a spiritual life? To answer this question let's evaluate specifically what some of our daily practices are. Then we will be able to see which "practices" are in accord with living spiritually and which ones are not. If the daily "practices" as a whole in your life are not based upon a spiritual foundation, then these "practices" themselves are obstacles to living a spiritual life.

Remember: that which we do the most is that which we do the best.

So let's look at what we do on a daily basis. The following may or may not represent what you do but I think you will get the point. On Monday morning many people get up shower and get ready for work. Statistics show that approximately 80% of all heart attacks occur between 9:00 a.m. and 11:00 a.m. on Monday morning. Therefore, it would seem that many people are frustrated with their jobs. They don't want to go to work and do the type of work that they are doing. Since people generally keep their jobs for the security, they are doing a job in a frustrated state. So on Monday mornings people begin their day by being frustrated which is it itself a practice. People then drive to a job that they don't want to go to, and often they drive in a manner that is very dangerous. They cut off other people and give each other the finger when this happens. This is known as road rage. People then become angry while driving to work. So now not only are they frustrated, but they are angry as well.

People then arrive at work frustrated and angry. What do they do when they get there? They spend a lot of time complaining. They complain about their boss, they complain about their co-workers, and often they complain openly about not liking their jobs. Then you have others who engage in gossip. These people look for something so that they could talk to others about it.

It's been my experience that this is the work environment for many people. At the end of the day, people rush to get home because they have not enjoyed work. But what happens during this rush to get home? More road rage—which by now is worse because everyone can't wait to get home. Unfortunately, the children must be picked up from school or daycare so not only do people rush to get home; they rush to pick up the kids as well.

In the race to pick up the kids, is anyone fitting in 'unwinding and relaxing from a hard day' to this schedule? No. You, as a parent, are thinking about what you're going to cook for dinner when you get home. You're also wondering how much homework you are going to have to help your child with. You really don't have time to unwind because of thinking about all of the things you still have to do. You know what this is called? Stress. So even during the drive home, you are stressed. This would not be classified as a severe form of stress but stress nevertheless.

Upon arrival home, you cook, eat, help the kids with their homework, clean up the kitchen, prepare the kids for school the next day, put them to bed and guess what? By now you are tuckered out. In fact, by now you are exhausted. By now you really don't have any energy and you still have not relaxed from your day. But if you have a partner in your life, your day is still not over. You may want to spend some quality time with your spouse, but the chances are that one of you will be exhausted from the day and won't be up to it. One of you may be that Energizer Bunny who keeps going and going and going. However, the other partner is often the opposite.

As a result the partner that wants the quality time often feels rejected even though it really is not personal. This is a rough way to live. Over time this feeling of rejection may lead to other problems in the relationship.

For those of you who are single, by the time the kids are off to sleep, you may either a) fall asleep as well because of your being tired, or b) you may feel lonely because you don't have anyone to share your life with. If you feel lonely then this feeling creates desire which creates a longing that you may not even acknowledge or be aware of. It can also unconsciously make you feel like you are missing out on something in life or that your life is not complete. Within yourself you become frustrated with being on your own instead of in a relationship.

So what is that we are feeling when we get home? Rushed.

During the whole course of an average day, what was "practiced"? Frustration, anger, gossiping, stress, rejection, and loneliness.

The following days of the week are similar. So it appears upon reflection that many people "practice" on a daily basis being frustrated, being angry, being stressed, feeling rejected and feeling lonely. Within this context where is the time for spiritual practice?

You may say that you go to church or the synagogue or the temple on a regular basis, and that may be true. You may also say that you know the precepts of what ever your religious doctrine is. You may know them well and be able to quote them. But what you do—what you "practice" on a daily basis—is being frustrated, being angry, being stressed, feeling rejected, and feeling lonely. Remember again, that which we "practice" most, is that which we do the best.

In the course of your day, how often do you love your neighbor as you love yourself? I mean how many people actually "practice" this when dealing with people in the course of their day? Isn't this a spiritual "practice?"

How many people "practice" not telling any lies at anytime no matter what? Isn't this a spiritual "practice?"

How many people "practice" being peaceful and contented in all circumstances? Don't many people say that they want their lives to be filled with peace and contentment? How then does one learn how to become peaceful and contented if one does not "practice" being peaceful and contented during the situations that develop in their life?

People did not suddenly become disenchanted with their jobs and with aspects of their life in general. These feelings developed over time, and through an unconscious "practice", people have become the 'things' that they actually dislike. So wanting peace, contentment, joy and so on, will only occur when a person begins "practicing" these attributes in their daily lives.

I believe in living life in a manner that promotes peace, joy, and contentment which, in turn, I believe creates an environment of happiness. However peace does not come by having a life in which there is no turmoil. Peace occurs by "practicing" being peaceful in the midst of turmoil. The more "practice" of peace during times of strife, the more peaceful one will become.

My father made his transition, passing away at the age of 64, and I immediately recognized that I needed to "practice" being peaceful during this time. This was extremely difficult. I, along with my cousin and aunt, made funeral arrangements for my father, and did all the things necessary for his funeral. Being peaceful in the midst of this emotional time frame was not easy. In fact, I was not peaceful for significant periods of time. But even in the midst of my crying or emotional outbursts, I internally "practiced" being peaceful: consciously and unconsciously, I understood that everything happens for a reason and that everything is in Divine order. This "practice" simultaneously created time periods in which I was able to be peaceful.

The more you "practice" being peaceful in all situations and all of life's experiences, the sooner you will reach a point in which you will be peaceful in all of life's situations. It takes "practice."

As long as a person continues to live their life in accordance with the "practice" of being angry, frustrated, stressed, jealous, envious, greedy, lonely, rejected and so on, one will continue to get better at making real these states. In this environment, it is impossible to live life in a spiritual manner no matter what religious ideology you hold. It is simply not possible. That's why the inability to recognize what we "practice" everyday keeps us from being able to live life spiritually. People wind up "practicing" those things that create the exact opposite of that which is desired.

Whatever your religious ideology, look within it for the guidelines on how to "practice" living life on a daily basis in a spiritual way. The guidelines are not there to be looked at and quoted once a week. They are to be "practiced" everyday, every moment of your life. The guidelines are right there in whatever scripture you study. However, what's the purpose of having guidelines if you don't "practice" them everyday? You cannot understand the spiritual aspect of your being until you begin the "practice" of living your life in a spiritual way on a daily basis. "Practicing" the tenets of your philosophy is the only way to begin the process of understanding the higher aspects of consciousness itself.

I study Neterianism which is the oldest religion and philosophy on Earth. It was founded and "practiced" by the Black African people who originally called their land Kemet which the Greeks later called Egypt. It was in Africa in the temples that the famed Greek philosophers Solon, Thales, Pythagoras, Socrates, Plato, and others studied and learned the philosophy which was later attributed to them.

These same Black African people are the people who built the pyramids and temples and great Sphinx as a result of the "practice" of Neterianism.[1] In fact, they are the people who laid the foundation for civilization as we know it. The 42 precepts of Maat are the "practices" of those great people that, over time, allowed them to build those monuments that people still look at with awe and wonder. However, every group has their own "practices." Every philosophy and religion has their "practices" so you must look to your own for guidance.

The problem is that people are so accustomed to being angry, frustrated, stressed, rejected, lonely, and so on that they don't even realize that they are. The problem is made worse because many people live life in the same way. As long as everyone around you is in the same condition as you, no one will appear to be out of the ordinary. Therefore everyone thinks that this state is normal **only** because everyone is the same. Not because it is normal. Since people think this *mistaken* **idea** is the reality, (constantly being angry, frustrated, jealous, envious, greedy, and lonely) it is believed that outer spiritual work (going to the mosque, going to church, going to the temple) is living spiritually. It is believed that talking to people about

---

[1] See page 136 for a detailed explanation on the "practice" of Neterianism.

81

salvation is "practicing" living a spiritual life. Well, talking to people about something is not the "practice" of it. You can be told about hitting a golf ball. That has nothing to do with whether or not the person telling you knew how to hit one, or even if that person knew what a golf ball looked like.

Many people do this outer work of spirituality. How many consistently do the inner work?

You may want to reflect on the inner aspects of spirituality whatever your religious ideology. Do you live it everyday? If you do not, are you "practicing" every moment to live the tenets of your ideology? Or are you talking about these tenets while you are still angry, still frustrated, still gossiping, etc?

Do you see how much of your energy is being wasted? Do you see how you are actually keeping yourself in a position in which you will always be talking about spirituality but not being able to enjoy the fruits of its "practice?"

What are the fruits of its "practice?" The things that everyone consistently says that they want: happiness, peace, contentment, joy and so on. These are virtuous qualities and these are the qualities that need to be "practiced."

When the "practice" of happiness is substituted for the "practice" of anger, a shift in consciousness happens.

When the "practice" of peace replaces the "practice" of frustration, a shift in consciousness happens.

When the "practice" of loving thy neighbor as you love thyself is substituted for talking about people behind their back, a shift in consciousness happens.

When the "practice" of contentment is substituted for the "practice" of jealousy, envy, greed, and the feeling of low self worth, a shift in consciousness occurs.

It is only when spiritual "practices" are in fact "practiced" by you in your daily life that you will be able to understand the subtle nature of Spirit. As long as life is lived according to the "practice" of anger, frustration, jealousy, envy etc., this way of being will sap all of your energy. It takes a lot of energy to be angry and frustrated. Have you ever noticed how tired you are after being angry at someone? It takes a lot out of you.

But when you master the "practice" of living life in accordance with the things you say you want out of life—happiness, peace, joy, contentment, etc.—then you will find within yourself renewed energy. You will find that people will see you differently. You will find that you will radiate, and people will be attracted to you. They won't know why but they will. You will then feel like a spiritual being having a human experience. You won't just say it. You will know it.

It is at this point that you will then be ready to "experience" the subtle nature of spirit. It is at this point that you will be able to understand the underlying truth in "all" religious doctrines. It is then that you will stop hating or disliking those who do not believe what you believe or "practice" what you "practice." You will be able understand the underlying basis of truth in all things. It is at this point that your full daily "practice" of spiritual life will completely substitute for the previous one. It is then that you will know that you are ready to understand through experience, what the purpose of life is.

"Practice" does make one perfect. Do you "practice" living your life in a spiritual manner in all situations and all conditions? If "practice" makes perfect, then consciously perfect the "practice" of living your daily life, moment by moment, in accordance with the precepts of your religious doctrine. You and the world will become a better place with "practice."

REFLECTION:

1   **Do YOU "see" how YOUR current Practices reinforce *mistaken* Ideas?**
2   **Does Practice Make Perfect?**

CHAPTER 7

WHO AM I REALLY?
(Who do you think you are?)

REFLECTION:

1   Are YOU the skin organ?
2   Are YOU a human?
3   Who do YOU think YOU are?

The previous chapter addressed <u>physical</u> "practices"—such as gossiping or lying—that reinforce accepted <u>mistaken</u> **ideas**. The following two chapters address purely <u>mental</u> "practices". These <u>mental</u> "practices" are internal. They are "thoughts" that reinforce previously accepted internalized **ideas.** Contrary to popular opinion, "thoughts" (or thinking) is an active process. Therefore thoughts and thinking are internal **actions**. The next two Chapters address "thoughts" that people have that reinforce previously accepted <u>mistaken</u> **ideas**.

Many people aspire to live life spiritually. However, many people don't know what living a spiritual life means. Some use the term spirituality interchangeably with the term religion. Those who speak about spirituality do not always clearly define what they mean when using the term. So discussion of spirituality can be confusing.

For clear understanding the reader should recall that, for purposes of this book, spirituality is defined as "**any practice which leads one to the answer of the question, "Who Am I"**. This question—and its answer—should be considered a philosophical question that can be answered through practice of a particular lifestyle.

For purposes of this book the reader should also note the following. There are two types of lives. A spiritual life and a human life. Before you can live a spiritual life, (before you can engage in practices that lead you to the answer of the question *Who Am I?)* you need to be keenly aware of what it is to live a human life.

The thought of what it means to be "human" should not be taken for granted or lightly. Although at first you may think that this term needs no explanation or thought—the contrary is true. You may think that waking up everyday and 'doing things' is what being human is all about.

I submit to you that this is a *mistaken* **idea**, and is very far from the truth. People often make statements such as "I am only human" and discuss themselves in terms of being human. Very few have ever actually given thought to what it means to be "human."

This distinction is very important and actually critical in being able to live a spiritual life. The common **idea** of what it means to be human is often intertwined with people's **idea** of who they are. This **idea** of who a person believes themselves to be differs from the philosophical question of "Who Am I". It is the **idea** of who a person believes themselves to be—in this case human—that is discussed in this chapter.

And it is this **idea** of what being human is that is an obstacle to living a spiritual life.

So what is the nature of being human? What do you think about when the word human is spoken? What comes to mind? What comes to mind if you were asked the question *Who am I*? Specifically who do you believe yourself to be? What is your **idea** of who you are?

To give a deeper mode of thought to the question, right now write down or think about the first five things that come to your mind when the question of "who are you" is posed.

Don't give long thought nor ponder it too long.

The first five things that come to mind, write those down on the following page.

What Are The First 5 Things That Come To Mind When I Ask You *Who Are You*?

Now let's examine what you have. When asked this question, many people give the following types of answers: Their name, age, and marital status. They may say they are the daughter of, or son of, so and so. They might indicate their race or ethnicity. If you asked a person what do they "see" when they imagine themselves, they would tell you that they "see" their skin. Did the five things that came to your mind when I asked you who you are mirror some of these answers?

Now let's look carefully and critically at these. First let's look at your name. Is your name *who you are*? Many people change their names but that in and of itself does not change the core essence of their being. Is your name an accurate reflection of who you are?

What about your age. Age is based on the idea that the world revolves around the sun every approximate 365 days. This time frame was then determined to be a time measurement. However, this method of selecting a time frame was an arbitrary choice. Years could be determined based upon how often the Sun revolves itself around the Milky Way galaxy. Years could be determined based upon the amount of time it takes the moon to travel around the Earth. So your present age is arbitrary. If you are "35" in our cycle of time and "350" in another, does that change the essence of who you are? Better yet, does it help you answer the question of who you are?

What about marital status? Does being single or being married have any reflection on the core aspect of who you are? You know the answer already.

And what about the biggest one of all, your skin. Many people when they think about themselves think automatically about their skin. Is the skin a fair reflection of who we are? Think about it. Remember 6th and 7th grade science class when you learned that atoms, when combined with other atoms, made up cells and these cells when combined with other cells make up organs? Do you recall learning this? What were some of the organs you learned about the body? You learned that the kidneys, lungs and heart were all organs. You were also taught which organ was the largest for a person:

the skin. So when you close your eyes and imagine who you are, if what you "see" is the skin organ, how come you don't see the heart, kidney or any other organ? It is because people have allowed themselves to believe an **idea** that is simply untrue. The *mistaken* **idea** that a person is their skin.

So I now ask you this: What does a person's name, age, ethnicity, and marital status all have in common? They are all descriptions of a person. Words that describe people are known as adjectives. If your **idea** of who you are is a description, an adjective…then what is the actual thing or noun that those adjectives are describing?

If you have been living your life with the **idea** that you are either an adjective or an organ, can you honestly say that you are in fact human? Is the essence of being human only adjectives? Is this essence an organ? If being human is more than that and if you have not lived life to discover what this more is, how have you actually been acting?

Are You An Adjective?
Are You An Organ?
Who Are You Really?

Let me give you an example. In the Disney movie "The Lion King", Simba the young lion cub was the son and heir to the throne of his father. When he was a small cub, his evil uncle killed Simba's father and tricked Simba into believing that he was responsible for it. So as a very young lion cub, Simba ran away and befriended other animals in the jungle. Simba **chose** to forget that he was the rightful heir to the throne. He was afraid of going back to battle his uncle for the throne. It was in the jungle that Simba grew up. He grew up though without any other lions around. So Simba never knew what it meant to be a lion. To survive he befriended a meerkat and warthog. He ate their foods and acted like them. He did everything but act like a lion. Simba acted like this because he did not remember who he was.

Needless to say, no matter how much he acted like other animals, it did not work. It took another lion—his childhood friend lioness Nala—to remind him that he was in fact a lion and heir to the throne. It was this lioness that convinced him to go home and regain what was rightfully his: the throne.

Nala provided Simba with an **idea** about himself that was different from what he had believed while growing up in the jungle. Simba <u>chose to forget</u> that he was heir to the throne. People, like Simba, innately know who they are. Through identification with **ideas** in their environment about who they are, people like Simba have also <u>chosen to forget</u> who they are innately. At some point, the reader may find that they too have a Nala in their life who has reminded them of who they are innately. Once the reader identifies with this new **idea,** they like Simba will do what is necessary to take back what is rightfully theirs. The throne which for the reader means the knowledge of Self.

Simba could not be a meerkat or warthog, because that isn't who he was. You, like Simba, may act for awhile like you're an adjective or an organ, but in time, like Simba, you too will have to face the reality of recognizing who you are really. The reality that one's **idea** of who they are is inaccurate.

"I'm Only Human"

This is another favorite chapter; because I often hear people use the term, "I'm only human" to mitigate times in which they were weak willed. When I had no money and wanted something, even though it would be difficult to pay it back, I charged it anyway and said "I'm only human." When people are on diets for serious health reasons, they have a piece of cake against doctors' orders and justify it by saying, "I'm only human, and you only live once." When a person smokes a cigarette and they know that smoking will kill them, they again justify it by saying, "I'm only human."

In other words: I'm going to enjoy life.

Maybe it's me, but I rarely hear people using the term "I'm only human" during times of power and strength. In fact it is my experience that when something powerful is done by a person, people tend to feel more than human. They feel proud and strong whereas people tend to feel human during times of weakness typically during times in which they could not control themselves. Why is this?

What is your experience? Think about it. When are the times that you are most likely to use the term "I'm only human?—during times of strength, or times of weakness?

If you evaluate these time frames, you will probably discover that your present **idea** about being human is not such a wonderful thing. If being human means one is weak willed and does not choose to exercise the ability of controlling themselves in one or many circumstances, why should anyone want to be like this? Wouldn't this mean that one was at the control of something or someone, and not in control of themselves?

When People Use The Term "I'm Only Human" They Are Typically in a Moment of Being Weak-Willed Or Not In Control of Themselves

Let me give you an example. When I was a youngster of about six my mother and father divorced. I look a lot like my father. So as I grew up, many people said to me: "You look just like your father." They would also say, "He's just like his father" if I did something that reminded them of him. That would have been okay if I had liked my father. But my father was a terrible father. In fact, at that time I could not stand him.

I was hurt and disappointed and this left an indelible mark on me. He walked out on us and never looked back. He was a terrible role model. He hung out with junkies and dope fiends and allowed me to engage in behaviors that were totally inappropriate for a child.

Anyway, as a result I did everything in my power to be different from my father. Even though I could not change looking like him, I could be different from him. I stayed in school and got great grades. I went to the top high school in my city. I went to college and became the first person in my family to graduate. I became the first to get a graduate degree by attending and graduating from law school. I did all of these things with an underlying motivation of trying to be different from my father.

This *desire* to distance myself from him was in fact *controlling me*. It was my motivation. It gave me the strength to keep on going when times were hard. This desire, however and my acting in conformity with it, was a time in which I was acting in a manner in which I was "only human." I was not in control of myself: instead, my desire to distance myself from my father was my control. This means that I was actually weak willed at that point, because I allowed something other than me to be in control of my actions.

I did not even realize that I was not in control of myself.

It was years later, and I mean years later—I had to be about 35 or 36—when I realized that my desire to be different from my father had to be let go. Sure, you could say that in this instance this desire had benefited me. I had two degrees and was doing okay. But who knows where I would have been had I been operating through life for me.

Anyway, it took me almost a year to let go from my mind my desire to do things to be different from my father. It became a crutch and I was actually afraid to let go because I believed that if I was not doing things to be different from him, I would not be able to do it myself. This is a sign of a weak will and it was a time for me in which I was "only human."

If you reflect on the times in which you use the term *I'm only human*, I think you will also find that it is used during times of weakness or during a time in which you exhibit a weak will. This inability to control yourself, and acting in a manner that you know is not good for you is indicative of a person who acts through instinct. There are other inhabitants in the world that act on instinct no matter what the circumstances, and those are our fellow animals. The difference is in our level of reasoning and rationalizing.

Animals do things entirely based upon instinct and learned behavior. They are biologically wired to do nothing else. They kill to eat when their stomach tells them to; they look to mate at certain times of the year when their body tells them to. This is all that they can do. People on the other hand have the ability to contemplate, reflect, and ponder. This is known as having an intellect. A person can choose to eat when they consider it time to eat. Not because they see a picture of a Big Mac or Whopper, but because it is time for them to give fuel to their bodies. This intellect can also be used to discern what type of foods should be placed in the body based upon nutritional value. When was the last time that you used your intellect before having a snack, lunch or dinner?

What use is an intellect if it is not going to be used?

Most people know the things that are good for them and those that are not. It is easy for a person to use the adage "I'm only human" so that they can cave in to their emotions instead of using their intellect and willpower to do what's in their best interest. If you are the type of person who uses the "I'm only human term" on more than a few occasions, then you are acting in accord closer with that of an animal, rather than that of the entity known as a human.

A Human Being Is One Who
Utilizes Their Ability to Ponder, Reflect and Contemplate
Before Making a Decision
And Then Has the Willpower
To Act in Conformity with that Decision

For purposes of this book, this heading above is the definition of what it means to be human: one who utilizes their ability to ponder, reflect and contemplate before making a decision—and then has the willpower to act in conformity with that decision.

According to my definition, there are very few people who would qualify as human. Living like this is not easy. Especially in a society that encourages people to be weak willed and also encourages them to not think for themselves but to let others think for them. It is much easier to respond to emotion and instinct than to think for yourself. However, the easy way is not the human way. It is the way of animals. As long as people choose to live their lives based on instinct they will never be able to live a spiritual life. You must be able to live a human life before you can live a spiritual one.

Many people have an **idea** that the essence of who they are is the skin organ. Many also have a negative **idea** of being human based upon the way the word is used. These **ideas** <u>form the essence of who people believe themselves to be</u>. People's entire way of being occurs as a result of the foundation of this thought. This/these thoughts are not empowering. In fact they are the opposite. They promote weak will.

92

You cannot achieve your dreams and do the impossible with an internal foundation of "I'm only human." It is unfortunate that people willingly adopt this **idea** that stands at the core of their very being. It is unfortunate for the person and it is also for the rest of society. A person with a different **idea** of who they are could develop a cure for cancer. A person with a different **idea** could solve the crisis of world hunger or poverty. A person with a different **idea** could figure out a way to establish peace on earth. These people could do this because their **idea** about themselves was more than just 'being human'. How much better society would be by having more people in our midst with a different **idea** of who they are?

Who are you really? Who do you think you are? Does this thought allow you to feel like you can be all that you can be? If not, ponder, reflect and analyze on a different **idea** about yourself. About who you are that **YOU** choose. Society is in need of you being all that you were designed to be right now! Choose this for yourself. If not for you then for everyone else.

REFLECTION:

1   Many students of religion verbally state that they are "Children of God." Are these statements mere words or do people 'really' believe it?

2   If the *Idea* that people are Children of God is true, what daily Practices are used to reinforce this *Idea*?

3   What daily Practices negate the belief?

CHAPTER 8

BRIDGING THE INTERNAL DISTANCE

REFLECTION:

1   You never miss the water until the well runs dry!

This chapter is a tribute to my father. It is written especially for those who have spent a childhood or significant portion of their life without their father around. Like many parents, my father and mother divorced when I was quite young. And like many others, my father spent very little time with me or my brothers and sister after the break-up. All of us felt the impact of his absence. At different moments in my life I felt <u>abandoned</u>. I felt like he <u>didn't care about me</u>. My self esteem suffered. I felt these emotions well through my late 30s and early 40s. I grew up very <u>angry</u> with my father. Over time, the anger changed to <u>resentment</u>. Later it became <u>disrespect</u>. And then it changed into a feeling of not caring about him or anything that happened to him.

My anger, resentment, and disrespect all happened when I had 'thoughts' about the situation that reinforced mistaken **ideas** that became real for me.

I had a *mistaken* **idea** that my father did not care for me. I had a *mistaken* **idea** that I was owed a better father than the one I had. These *mistaken* **ideas** created an environment in which "thoughts" could develop that reinforced the validity of the *mistaken* **idea**.

The thought of <u>abandonment</u> reinforced the *mistaken* **idea** that he did not care. The thought of <u>upset-ness</u> led to the emotion of anger, resentment, and disrespect. These thoughts reinforced the *mistaken* **idea** that I was owed a father better than the one I had.

The thoughts of abandonment and upset-ness were <u>mental</u> "practices" that reinforced the so-called reality of my circumstance.

I wrote this chapter because I want everyone who has had this same experience to realize something that I did not realize until it was too late.

- The **REALITY** is that our fathers did the best they knew how to do.
- The **REALITY** is that our fathers would have done better if they could have.
- The **REALITY** is that our fathers wanted what was best for us.

No one was promised that their life would follow a self-created script written typically as children. The **REALITY** is that no matter what your present relationship or circumstance with your father (or mother) is like, your experience of that parent—and all that it is and all that it is not—has contributed in a positive way to you being who you are today. This experience of your father (or mother) has been and is in fact something positive. You are the sum total of your experiences. The not-so-good experiences of your father (or mother) have shaped you in the same ways as every so-called good experience with others. This may sound strange but this is something that I have personally realized.

As you recall from previous chapters, my father suddenly and unexpectedly died of a stroke while I was writing this book. He was 64 years old. In one instant, I no longer had anyone to be mad at. No one to resent. And most importantly, I could no longer unconsciously hope that I would be able to have the type of relationship from him that I wanted.

I cried a great deal during the week preparing for his funeral. But my tears were not tears of remorse for losing someone that I was close to or fond of. My tears formed on the fact that I knew at that moment that it was over. My hopes of a relationship with him were gone forever.

I cried because it wasn't fair. I was a good kid. Did the right things. And now my hopes for having the type of relationship that I wanted with my father were gone forever. *Why me*? I demanded.

I cried also because I realized that all of these years, all of my anger at him did one thing, and one thing only. It KEPT me from being in a position of having ANY type of relationship with him. With all of my anger and resentment, I kept him at a distance. I became the instrument by which I was prevented from having ANY type of relationship with him. Granted, he did not live with or close to us. But the distance I am referring to is the internal distance. When I did see him I was cold. This is the distance I am referring to. I did it to myself.

Sure, his conduct and actions angered me. But my reaction to his conduct and actions was in fact the cause of me turning him off internally. It was this realization that brought me the most pain, and the most tears, because I realized to a large degree that I had done a good portion of this to myself.

I wrote this chapter for those of you whose fathers or mothers are still in the land of the living. You still have time to share some type of experience with them. For you it's not too late.

I decided to include this chapter partly because of two experiences that happened to me when I got back to work after burying my father. Below you will find the tribute that I read to my father at his funeral. I read this to about four or five people at work. A couple of my colleagues thought that I should print it in some form. I gave thought to this idea. However, it was the experience I had with another co-worker that sealed it.

I have a colleague who had a wonderful relationship with their father while growing up. The relationship was solid. It was in the later years that the father-child relationship began to deteriorate, once my colleague had become an adult. My colleague's father and mother divorced and my understanding is that at this point, things began to sour in the father/child relationship. My colleague was an adult when the divorce of the parents happened.

My colleague was deeply hurt by what had transpired. We had talked about this prior to my father making his transition. I read the tribute to my father to this colleague and we both wound up crying. I told my colleague to not be like me. I told my colleague that there was still time to have some type of relationship with their father—even if it wasn't the type of relationship that they may have wanted.

My time with my father was up, and no matter how much I wanted something else, I couldn't get my father back. But for my colleague and those of you reading these words, you still have time.

What follows is the tribute to my father that I read at his funeral. It holds realizations that occurred to me AFTER he made his transition. These realizations upon reflection would have served me well had I had them prior to his death. It is my hope that they may serve you well if you can act on them before the transition of your father (or mother).

Thanks Dad!

Dad knew he wasn't going to be able to attend the family reunion in July so he brought us together today instead.

Thanks Dad!

There is a reason for everything. Why do people die? Because they are born. Everyone's days are numbered the second they are born. Why do they die when they do? Two reasons: First, their experience as a human being is no longer necessary. Second, because the experience of them for their family and friends is also complete.

To my brothers and sister: Do not mourn because we won't get to have the experience we may have wanted from our father. We all got the experience we needed. We are stronger now. We are resilient. We have good hearts. We are great people. We got the experience that we needed from our father to make us the people we are today, and that is a wonderful thing. Know in the depths of your heart that our father loved us a great deal. Know from the depths of your hearts, that he did the best he knew how to do. Know from the depths of your hearts, that if he could have done better he would have.

So Dad, I take this moment to thank you. Thank you for being just the way you were. It allowed me to be who I am today and I am a <u>great</u> man! For that Dad, I thank you.

Thanks Dad for providing in your death the opportunity for me to share and spend time with my brothers and sister in a manner of love and support. This experience has made me closer to each one of them, especially my sister, and without your transition, this would not have happened at this

moment in time.

Thanks Dad for bringing me up close and personal to my family, your siblings, my uncles and aunts, and cousins in a way that I have never experienced. I have spent more time with certain members of my family during your transition than I ever have. I have gotten to know them and they have gotten to know me.

Now Dad, you know you left us without your house being in order. (Dad died without life insurance) This made an already difficult circumstance much harder for me personally. But in retrospect Dad, I thank you for that too. I thank you because I found out that my cousin (Lou)[2] has a heart of gold. That without being asked, he was willing to do anything in his power to help me and his mother in this time. Thanks Dad for allowing me to get to know (Lou's) mother, your sister, my Aunt (Mabel) who was known as your partner/slash mother. I see why you two were close. She's had your back and she too has a heart of gold. (my cousin Lou and his mother, my Aunt Mabel were a tremendous help in the funeral arrangements of my father.)

Thanks Dad for allowing me to get to know my cousin (Aset) who will forever be to me like an older sister and also her husband and their daughter (Sesheta). I found that (Aset) and I have much in common. A bond like that of an older sister and younger brother. For that Dad I thank you.

Finally Dad, I want to thank you for allowing me to feel more like a member of this family during this week, than at anytime in my life. The myriad of ways in which all of you have provided support for my brothers and sister and to me personally during this time of strife—I am eternally grateful for.

So Dad, I know that things happen for a reason. Ultimately I don't know what the reason is for your transition at this

---

[2] (   ) Names in parentheses have been changed.

time. But I do know that I am thankful that you are my father. And I am thankful to you Dad, for being just the way you were!

For those of you reading this that have experienced having a father or mother similar to mine, I beseech you to reflect upon the following: What kind of person are you today?

No matter how upset you may be, no matter how angry you may be, no matter what your present life circumstance, you are still able to read these words. Therefore, you still have much life to live and much to live for.

I realized through my father's death that his absence from my life was just as influential on me and the way I turned out as a man and adult as any hoped-for experience could have been. I turned out alright. My experience of my father helped MAKE me who I am today. I wouldn't trade who I am today for anything in the world. Could I be better? Yes. Could I be worse? Yes. Do I wish that my experience of my dad was different? Of course.

This chapter is written for those who still have a dad around that you may still be mad at, hurt by, or upset with. Had I accepted my father unconditionally at any point in my younger years, my experience with him could have been different and would have been different.

I mentioned previously that my dad came to Detroit last summer and stayed for about three weeks. You may recall that I really didn't want to see him because I was still mad and hurt. I fooled myself into believing that I had forgiven him. Because of this so-called forgiveness, I visited him for about a couple of hours while he was in town.

However, I was very distant. Had I known at that time that this was going to be my last time with my dad FOREVER, I am sure that my disposition and demeanor would have been different.

I submit to you that had I thought one year before—two years before—five years before—that March 23, 2006 would be the last time that my father would be alive, I know I would have been different with him. I now realize that had my actions been different, I would have created a different environment. We would have been able to communicate.

So reflect upon these words. Recognize and realize that your father or mother has their own set of issues and problems that contributed towards them being the way that they were with you. No one wants to be a terrible person to another—especially to their own children. For whatever reason, parents like mine and parents that were far worse than mine could not do any better. Recognize that you probably will never have the type of relationship with your parent that you have imagined. That is not a bad thing! An imagined relationship is *illusory!* It is not real. It only exists in your mind.

Unfortunately, there is a group of people who have parents that did horrendous types of things to them. Things that are not explainable. Things that appeared to be done by choice. These parents often suffered from some type of emotional or psychological problem- emotional and/or psychological issues that had nothing to do with their children. For people with parents like this, there is only one type of relationship that is advisable. A relationship that shows you that the conduct inflicted upon you by them was not your fault. A relationship which allows you to see that the problem rests in them, not you. This will allow you to let go of the anger, hurt and other emotions. However, actually spending time with this type of parent is not advisable.

For those of you with parents who do not suffer from severe emotional or psychological problems understand that you can create a type of relationship with your parent that will bridge the internal distance. You can have a better relationship with them if you accept them as they are today and let go of your *mistaken* **ideas** of how things should have been. They did not know how to be better with you. If they did, they would have done it by now.

No one wants to be in the midst of an unfortunate circumstance. It is especially difficult for children who grow up in a dysfunctional home environment. However if you reflect upon those people in society who have risen to the top, often you will find that they too had to overcome dysfunctional or even abusive parental or home conditions. There is a saying that says, "things that don't kill you make you stronger." You are stronger today as a result of the experience. Shift your focus from what happened **to** you (victimhood), to I made it through an awful circumstance (control). Don't focus on the negative because they have gotten enough space through your anger, resentment, frustration and possibly your own emotional or psychological problems. Let them go. Based upon your experience, instead ask yourself the following: in what way/s can you manifest a different way

100

of being that will be helpful to others and society as a whole?

Your parent does not have to die before you can realize that you turned out ok in spite of the experience. Like I said previously, I am a great man today. ALL of my experiences, the good and not so good made me who I am today.

Do something different than I did. Don't let your parent die before you accept them as they are unconditionally. Accept them right now while they are alive. Accept them right now while you still have time to have lunch with them. Accept them right now, while they still have time to get to know their grandchildren. Accept them right now while you still have time to tell them that no matter what happened, you still love them for being your parent. Without parents you are not here. Accept them now while they are alive.

There is only one reason for writing a eulogy and my preference today is to never have had a reason to write one for my father. Acceptance of my father after he died was good for sure. But I would gladly trade places with any of you who still have your parents around today. I would accept him today unconditionally and would be glad for it.

FOR ALL OF YOU WHO MAY NOT BE READY TO SAY THIS TO YOUR FATHER, I WILL SAY IT FOR YOU:

THANKS DAD FOR BEING JUST THE WAY YOU ARE/WERE!

REFLECTION:

1   **Could YOUR Life be better?**
2   **Could YOUR Life be worse?**
3   **No matter what the circumstances of the past, YOU turned out great.**
4   **Adversity makes one strong. YOUR circumstances have made YOU strong. Now YOU are equipped to do GREAT THINGS!**
5   **Life does not typically give one what they want. Life gives you what you NEED!**

"Do Not Allow What You Think,
Or The Way You Think To
<u>*Limit*</u>
What You Think,
Or The Way You Think!"

-By: Anpu Waset

SECTION III

OBSTACLES & WAYS OF BEING IN MALE/FEMALE RELATIONSHIPS

Obstacles are **ideas** that people have forgotten are **ideas.** They are now accepted as true and factual. These **ideas** then become the person's *'reality'*. This phenomenon creates problems for a person because identifying with the **idea** creates a fixed and rigid mindset. The acceptance leaves no room for any other possibility or **idea**. The **idea** becomes an obstacle because the possibility of a new way of thinking is not accepted.

Ways of Being are **practices** which first enforce and over time reinforce that the specific **idea** is real. **Practices** can be physical or mental:
- Physical *practices* are outward actions such as talking and moving your body;
- Mental *practices* are internal—the thoughts that people have.
- ALL *practices* over time help you forget that the original **idea** was just that—an **idea**.

The Relationships chapter in this section combines *obstacles* AND *ways of being* within male/female relationships. The chapter highlights the common **ideas** and **practices** in relationships—**ideas** and **practices** that lead to the demise of the relationship. Present ideas about male/female relationships do not foster healthy and successful relationships. Present **ideas** actually foster the opposite: relationships that either end quickly through divorce or produce unhappiness, frustration and resentment.

If people do not divorce, these **ideas** and **practices** many times result in infidelity. Unlike previous chapters, a brief solution is given at the end of the Relationships chapter. You don't have to adopt the solution to help yourself in your present or future relationship. With a firm grasp of the **ideas** and **practices** common in relationships today, you are in a good position to choose with your mate a new **idea** and new *way of being* which will allow your relationship to prosper unlike most others in mainstream society.

CHAPTER 9

"RELATIONSHIPS"
(male/female)

REFLECTION:

1   Do YOU know anyone who has married and lived happily ever after?
2   Is the *Idea* that people marry and live happily ever after an *idea* that is ever true?
3   Does this Idea work?
4   Are there other *Ideas* about Relationships which can be practiced?

Have you ever heard the phrase "Why do fools fall in love?" It is appropriate that this phrase be kept in mind when exploring the wonderful yet chaotic or maybe chaotic yet wonderful world of male-female relationships.

A relationship is something that almost everyone wants, but once involved in, many cannot tolerate. It is the exact movement of opposites. At first you want a person then you don't. You leave them or they leave you. You then see someone else, you want them, you pursue them, and eventually you get them.

Then the process repeats itself. You don't want this new person, they don't want you and the process continues over again. Hopefully, each relationship is actually over prior to the "you see someone new, you like them, they like you cycle." This cycle is the same for both men and women but how it happens makes it appear that there is a difference. This 'difference' of the same cycle is probably what inspired "men are from Mars, women are from Venus". Again men and woman go through the same cycle. They just manifest these cycles in different ways.

This chapter will address **ideas** and *practices* about male/female relationships that doom them to failure. These **ideas** and *practices* are societal so most people are affected by them in the same way. It is the **ideas** and *practices* about relationships that create environments conducive for a great deal of stress, heartache, and pain.

These characteristics are not typically immediately noticed or seen. These are characteristics that appear one, two, three, four, five or more years after the relationship has begun…once the novelty wears off.

My goal is to help you become a bit more aware of your underlying present **ideas** on relationships and how this **idea** impacts the relationship itself. In essence does your **idea** about what relationships are contribute, and lead to, a happy, long lasting and fulfilling one—or does it create the exact opposite? A relationship that is short-lived and unfulfilling.

If it creates the former then read no further and move directly to the last chapter. If it creates the latter, then an alternative will be discussed. Namely, developing a new **idea** and *practice* about relationships that is wholly different from those you have presently. An **idea** and *practice* that you and your mate consciously decide to utilize at the beginning of a potential relationship.

The following will be discussed.

1.   The dynamics of the courting games that people play.

2.   The **ideas** people have about Relationships.

3.   The practices which reinforce those ideas.

4.   How the **ideas** and *practices* doom the Relationship from its beginning.

5.   A new **idea** and *practice* that will allow a couple to have the type of relationship that all strive for—a relationship that is fulfilling.

A <u>fulfilling relationship</u> is much different than the typical relationship of today. Our lives involving partners or lovers are permeated with much stress, hurt, resentment and definitely frustration. There are many facets to this topic so the question is asked:

WHY DO FOOLS FALL IN LOVE?

I would venture to say that it is totally accurate to describe people who fall in love as fools just like the song by Frankie Lymon. Why is this an accurate description? According to *Divorce Magazine*, as a percentage of marriages, the divorce rate in the USA is 49%. This is consistent with the divorce rates of the United Kingdom which is 53%, Canada at 45%, and France at 43%. In the United States according to *Psychology Today*, 60% of remarriages fail. This is consistent with those of the United Kingdom which according to their Office of National Statistics say over 60% of couples divorce the second time around. Look around at the people that you know who have been married longer than two years. How many first time marriages that you are aware of end in divorce? What about the second time marriages?

I don't know about you, but I know of very few things with success rates this low that people are jumping at the chance to do. Not only are people anxious to marry, they seem to feel like they are missing out on something if they are not married.

Would you drive a car the first time if you knew you had a 50% chance that you were going to wind up injured? Well, that's what happens to many people who divorce. They get hurt. They become injured. Hurt and injured in ways often much worse than a physical injury. A broken arm heals in approximately a month or two depending upon one's age and the nature of the break. Reset the arm if necessary, put a cast on it and very soon it's healed like new. A broken heart may take years to heal. For some of us, it never completely heals.

Although it is often said that time heals all wounds, emotional injury to your sense of self-esteem and worth can be irreparable. This type of injury can be permanent because people do not recognize this as an injury.

Would you drive a car the second time if you knew you had over a 60% chance that you would get hurt? This is what people do who marry a second time and divorce. They wind up hurt also. This may be a simple example, but think about it for a moment. Is there any activity that you would do the first time in which there was a 50% chance that you would be hurt, and then on the second attempt, there would be a 60% chance of injury? Probably not. This is why you could consider people to be foolish when it comes to affairs of the heart. But even knowing the probable outcome at the beginning, people still jump in anyway.

DYNAMIC # 1
A "FLOWER OF GOD"

And guess what? I know this is so because in my life it has happened to me on more than one occasion. I have been in situations when I have met a woman and, during that first encounter and even after meeting her, I felt so good I thought I was about to rise up and float away on Cloud Nine!

Have you ever met a person and everything just clicked instantly? You say a few words if you're a man and the woman is immediately interested? Or if you're a woman he says a few words to you, you look him over from head to toe, you size him up, and you are immediately interested?

And even though very few words are spoken, much is 'said' loud and clear through the chemistry? Then from there everything just develops so easily. You spend some time together and whether you say a little or a lot, the feeling is euphoric and the feeling makes you feel like you are on top of the world? Has this ever happened to you?

It's like seeing a flower bloom—a Flower of God—once the rays from the sun touch it. The rays make this flower radiate and glow with a heavenly air. Do you know what I'm talking about?

So yes, an argument can be made that only fools fall in love and it is understandable why. It just feels so good!

This is the main reason that people disregard the statistics—this euphoric feeling. The euphoric feeling takes over and you believe that this could be the one. No one thinks about anything else at this time. In some ways it's like being in a trance. A good trance—because it just feels so good. So good that it is hard to fight the feeling. Why fight it? Just go with it and enjoy it people say. This type of feeling is the first relationship dynamic at play that makes people foolish in the first place.

Of course it's foolish because you know that the feeling never lasts. Most people will consciously state that they are aware that the euphoric feeling is short lived. However, unconsciously, people still long to have the euphoric feeling. Many people are *in love with the **idea** of being in love!* This is especially true of women but is true of men also. In this case people have the euphoric feeling twice simultaneously. First with the thought of falling in love and second, when they meet a person who they think is "the one".

The **idea** of being in love makes you giddy and makes your heart beat faster. The thought of being in love in the mind is often no different from being in love itself. The feeling is no different. This is a dangerous mindset for both men and women. It is dangerous because a person who "sees" love through this euphoric feeling **idea** has produced a mind that is rigid and inflexible. A rigid and inflexible mind does not allow you to "see" clearly.

This type of mind will not allow you to see a new object of your affection in a true light. A person *in love with the **idea** of being in love* will gravitate towards people who support the self-created image that is equated with love. You may see your Prince Charming as dressing well, with a lot of money, looking a particular way, and so on. As soon as the self-created image appears in your mind, the *in love with being in love **idea*** kicks in and you will not see any negative qualities of this person. You will not see that this person may be a liar. You won't notice their insecurity. You will not see that the person may not be stable. None of this will be seen because your mind has become fixed and inflexible on the self-created **idea** of *love.* This **idea** blinds you to the reality—the person is no good—and makes you believe that this new person is the one. All this simply because they fit the profile of what the person should look or be like according to your *in-love **idea*** that you created in your mind.

It should be no surprise that people burdened with this way of thinking are generally attracted to the same types of people over and over again. And it should be no surprise that those with this mindset rarely, if ever, get the love that they have imagined. People with this mindset never give up hope that they will meet the 'right' person. They look up and ten, twenty—or more—years pass, but they never get the "love" that they have always wanted.

Keep in mind that the *in love with the **idea** of being in love* syndrome is in actuality a longing for the euphoric feeling. This longing is based upon the unconscious *mistaken* **idea** that this euphoric feeling should always be there. It is this euphoric feeling that people long for in the first place. It is this euphoric feeling they look for when they search for a mate. And it is this euphoric feeling that makes a person feel like they have found the 'one' each and every time this feeling is triggered.

It is the unconscious desire—**idea**—to have a constant euphoric feeling that makes people foolish when it comes to love. Foolish because everyone knows of couples whose relationship sours once this euphoric feeling has gone. Instead of seeing the beauty of that Flower of God at all times, we begin to see problems of the person instead and their baggage.

Unfortunately, people do not reflect on things so they don't realize how a start to a relationship that feels so good can sour quickly and go the opposite direction in just a few weeks, months or years. Reflection allows you to understand clearly how people go from that high place to the low one. Once this dynamic is understood, people can act differently and prevent the relationship from souring. The dynamic itself can change based upon your understanding of it.

We will now discuss some of the other dynamics that make people foolish when falling in love.

DYNAMIC #2

PEOPLE ARE UNCONCIOUSLY TAUGHT FROM CHILDHOOD TO VIEW LOVE A SPECIFIC WAY

To fully understand this dynamic, watch cartoons or television shows with your four- to eight-year-old child for approximately two to three hours. If this is not possible, recall the television shows that you watched when you were that age. While watching, take notice of the shows in which the topic of love came up. When you see or recall a show like this, then watch for how the love scenario plays out. They always happen in the same way.

Boy likes girl. Boy does not tell girl he likes girl. Girl likes boy. Girl does not tell boy she likes him. Boy and girl somehow find themselves around each other. Boy smiles a lot around girl. Girl smiles a lot around boy. Boy wants to kiss girl. Girl wants boy to kiss her. At the end of the show, depending on how old are the two, boy and girl seal the show with a kiss as lovely music plays in the background. Boy and girl walk away holding hands as the sun shines bright in the background.

This is my recollection. Now watch for yourself and see how many of these shows have the same type of storyline when the topic is love. Also notice the type of music that plays while the love 'feeling' is happening. You may be surprised to see that almost every show that deals with infatuation for kids has this same basic storyline. So from the time that people are boys and girls in this society from the ages as young as four, this is what children are learning about love. This forms the initial **idea** about what children initially think about love. An **idea** by the way which is *mistaken.*

What happens as these children get older? The movies add a bit more music, a bit more violence, and of course now sexual innuendo, and then sex. But what happens to the story lines about love? They stay the same! The only thing that changes is that as people get older in the movies, men start coming to the rescue of the woman while she is in distress.

I remember the movie "Pretty Woman" with Julia Roberts and Richard Gere. Julia Roberts plays the part of a prostitute who Richard Gere picks up while he is in a particular city on business. As a prostitute, Julia's character still wants her knight in shining armor for she desires the common *mistaken* **idea** about love. She wants to marry and live happily ever after. Richard Gere's character falls in love with the prostitute, and at the end of the movie, he travels to her home in his white limousine—the modern day version of a white horse—with candy and flowers. And he proposes to her. Richard Gere's character <u>knows</u> that she is a prostitute. He has already utilized her services. After the proposal she of course says yes, and the movie ends with them riding off into the sunset on the white horse—err, the white limousine—as the sun shines in the background while happy music plays.

<u>Even a **_prostitute_** gets her knight in shining armor to come to her rescue and take her away to live happily ever after!</u>

So, from childhood to adulthood people are given a steady *mistaken* diet of what romance Hollywood-style looks like. Many of us grow up believing that this is how romance looks and ***should be!*** People actually grow up unconsciously expecting that their relationship should look like what they keep seeing in the movies. As adults, the **idea** fully develops and becomes *reality*. This **idea** is looked for in a relationship and anything short of this look makes one feel that something is missing. This *mistaken* **idea** is looked for and expected. When it doesn't materialize people long for something more. Longing becomes frustration which becomes upset-ness which becomes resentment which leads to the host of problems common in relationships. Subconsciously, women still desire a knight in shining armor and men still desire a damsel in distress.

Unfortunately, most Hollywood movies end with the couple riding off into the sunset, immediately after the proposal or immediately after the wedding while nice music plays in the background. None of the movies discuss what happens two, four, five, seven, eight or more years later after the couple has married. People are fools for falling in love when they do not FULLY recognize that their **ideas** about romance and relationships will not be like it is in the movies.

DYNAMIC #3
PEOPLE HAVE BAGGAGE FROM GROWING UP THAT DOES NOT MANIFEST UNTIL THEY ARE MARRIED

The next dynamic that makes people foolish when falling in love is the failure to recognize how ones' particular upbringing and environment shaped their views on how male/female relationships should be. For far too many of us, that upbringing is often dysfunctional. For example, in a household in which a person was always called "dumb" or "stupid", this person will manifest this feeling. Even worse, this person will attract others who will reinforce that belief. Once people become conditioned in a particular way based upon their upbringing they often unconsciously attract people that keep them in that same dynamic. Of course this type of thought about oneself—that one is stupid or dumb—is not helpful. It is even worse when ones' mate begins treating them in this manner. People attract others who reinforce positive and negative attributes of themselves.

Therefore, if a person grows up unconsciously thinking that they are stupid, it is just a matter of time before they find a mate who will act in accordance with that belief.

This is another reason people are attracted to the same types over and over again. They unconsciously attract others who will reinforce the strongest unconscious aspects in themselves no matter whether they are positive or negative. No matter how many different relationships they become involved in, they will continue to attract the same type of people. This is because this person has not yet realized their own baggage from their long-ago past, nor have they taken the necessary steps to deal with it.

Now the stupid/dumb example is an extreme one. But there are many other characteristics stemming from ones' upbringing and environment that one brings into the relationship. This is called baggage. Unfortunately, baggage is not evaluated before dating. It should be evaluated at the beginning but is overlooked because the 'feel-good feeling' is so strong. Even if both people were looking for this baggage, it would be difficult to see past the fog of the euphoric feeling. However it is possible and is actually to be encouraged.

The realization of your baggage and your mate's baggage at the start of the relationship—if handled properly—is the key towards having a wonderful and fulfilling relationship. This realization could act like a form of glue that brings a new couple closer together. The inability to recognize you and your mate's baggage at the start of the relationship and its potential consequences on the relationship itself keeps people as fools who fall in love.

The inability to recognize baggage at the beginning of a relationship is very unfortunate. It is this so-called baggage of both people that will create major future challenges for the couple during the relationship. These challenges—if handled by societal standards—doom the relationship to failure.

There are many types of baggage that people bring into relationships that are not realized. Women want security so they may talk in terms of a man having to have money. Money is actually security. This is a form of baggage. Men want wives who will take care of them. Make them dinner and make them feel like a man. This is a form of baggage. Other types of baggage include but are not limited to having predefined ideas about the proper roles in the relationship. The man wants the final say on all matters. However, the woman may make more money than him, so she thinks she should make all the decisions. One person may be domineering and the other passive. One may be romantic and the other a couch potato. All of these things are baggage that, in and of themselves, are no big deals. However, in the context of living "happily ever after" none of this baggage is helpful.

It is not helpful because people get stuck in acting in conformity with the baggage. Their reality of how the relationship is going is based on the view clouded by the baggage. For example, a woman may have the baggage of thinking that a "real man" is a man that fixes things around the house. She may have this baggage because of an upbringing in which her father always fixed things in her home as she grew up. In the context of her relationship, if her husband is a college graduate who grew up without a father who never learned how to fix anything, she may begin to "see" him thru the lens of this "real man image." Over time she may begin to view him as "less of a man."

So the baggage is not bad in and of itself, it is how people allow the baggage to 'cloud' their view of their mate or relationship that proves to be detrimental.

DYNAMIC # 4, 5, 6, 7..............
THE LIST OF BAGGAGE BASED ON ENVIRONMENT AND UPBRINGING, IS EXHAUSTING

There are other dynamics based upon a person's upbringing that play themselves out, once that person is involved in a relationship. Did a person grow up with both parents in the household? If so, what role did each parent play? You can best believe that a person, who saw a defined role growing up, will expect to live out that same role when they marry. Was a person a product of a single-parent household? If the person is a male who grew up in a single-parent household headed by his mother, then this male probably grew up without any male role model. His *idea* of how he should be in a relationship is based on what he saw on TV, in the movies, and on the streets. None of these are places to be trained in how to be a man. A male like this or a female raised without a father figure are like lightning bolts

113

around metal. It is just a matter of time before it strikes, meaning you don't know what type of man or woman this person will be in the relationship before it happens.

There are many other things that could be added to the above. The list is exhausting and could be discussed for quite some time. However, what's important to understand is that it is difficult at best and sometimes impossible at worst, to know before a relationship begins how a person's upbringing and environment will play itself out in the actual relationship. A woman who grew up seeing her mother abused may attract men who abuse her. However, she may not. You really don't know. A man who grew up without his father around could turn out to be a great father, while it is just as plausible that he could turn out being a terrible one. Again, this uncertainty makes dating and relationships difficult. Especially if you don't factor this in at the beginning and plan for this before it manifests in a way that will lead to strife.

There is more that could probably be discussed about these dynamics but I will leave it here for now. To bring this first point related to what got people to the place in which they are many times fools for falling in love, we can summarize it as follows:

- First it feels sooooooo gooooood! We become hypnotized by this feeling and we simply stop thinking.

- Second we are unconsciously taught by society to think that this good feeling is Love in a relationship setting. We think that Love in a relationship will be like it is in the movies. People think that as soon as they get the relationship, they will live happily ever after.

- Third, people don't give any thought to how their upbringing has influenced their thoughts on relationships.

- Fourth, even if thought was given to one's upbringing, people generally don't recognize the effects of this upbringing until they are actually involved in the relationship...which is by then too late.

THE COURTING PHASE OF THE RELATIONSHIP IS SIMILAR TO THAT OF A DRUG ADDICT

Now let's change gears a bit and discuss how the courting of a person also makes people foolish. By courting I mean the process of meeting a person and then dating them. It was mentioned earlier how I have felt before when meeting a woman. Do you remember the way you felt when the same thing happened to you and that person that you really liked, reciprocated and liked you as well? Did it make you feel like you were on top of the world? It is this feeling that also makes people fools to fall in love. This feeling should be distinguished from the *in love with being in love **idea***. Both feelings are euphoric. However, the former occurs <u>before </u>a person meets someone. The euphoric feeling being referred to now occurs <u>after</u> the potential person of one's dreams is met.

This feeling is foolish because it doesn't last. It is temporary. Sometimes it lasts for two years. Typically it's about a year or a year and half, and then all of a sudden it's gone. After the love is gone, people then continue to either long for that feeling again, or they search to get that feeling again. People long for it from their present relationship if they're still involved in one, or if single, search for the feeling through meeting another person. That's why people say "If I find the right person I will get involved in a relationship." The right person is the person who makes them have that 'puppy-love feeling'. It is that puppy-love feeling that they are longing for.

Over the course of a person's life, they find this puppy-love again in different relationships to varying degrees but what is consistent is that it never lasts. If a couple is dating, once the feeling ends the couple breaks up. If the couple marries then once the puppy-love fades, generally problems creep up in the relationship. No matter what the status of a relationship, people either continue looking for that feeling if they are not in a relationship, or they long to regain that feeling if they are involved in one.

There are other types of individuals that exhibit this type of behavior. Drug addicts. They use a drug for the first time and because their bodies are not used to it, they get very high. They then continue using drugs longing to get that same original high but to no avail. They get high for sure, but it is rarely the same as it was the first time. Did you know that these puppy-love feelings and the addictive tendency all occur in the same parts of the brain? Any addiction—whether it is smoking, drinking, sex, greed, eating for pleasure, any of these things—if you looked at the brain when any of these were happening, you would find the same area of the brain functioning at each time any of these were occurring.

So in essence, people search for relationships because they are addicted to the puppy-love feeling. They keep looking and searching over and over again, fall in love, fall out of love, fall in love again, fall out of love again. And all the while they are thinking that the 'right person' will permanently solve this dilemma. The more this behavior is done, the more ingrained we teach ourselves that a special person exists. This keeps us in a vicious cycle that prevents us from being able to critically look at what in fact it is that we are doing to ourselves.

So in the courtship ritual, in fact what is happening is that we are chasing a fix. Although we know that the high won't last forever, or a long time either, it is chased anyway, because it feels so good while it lasts. How foolish is that?

Now go a bit further. Think about what happens when the courtship changes from the dating to the serious relationship, or better yet, marriage. Well recognize first that many people expect for the puppy-love feeling to continue. Even though intellectually many will tell you that they know this feeling doesn't last, unconsciously they expect it to. This is because of what people have been taught about love. So this is the first change. The feel-good novelty wears off. Now what do you get when the novelty wears off? You get to see all of the things that you chose to overlook while you were feeling so good. Did you know that drug addicts once high forget about eating, sleeping, and a host of things? They live in a place of being on top of the world in their eyes while they are high. As long as they are high, everything is wonderful. It is when the high wears off that they see that they have lost weight and have bags underneath their eyes. It's no different in a relationship.

Have you been in love and all you did was think about the other person? You did not have an appetite while thinking about this person. You could not concentrate fully at work because you could not wait until later on when you would see this person. While feeling the puppy-love—the high— your mate can do no wrong. It's cute if he leaves his underwear on the floor.

116

It's no big deal that she doesn't want to cook. If he can't fix a doorknob, what does that mean? I love him. If she doesn't put out whenever I want it's okay. I love her. All of these scenarios apply equally to either person. While in love—when high—none of this matters. When the puppy-love leaves—when the high wears off—all of these stop being cute. That's when they start becoming problematic.

"YOU BEEN TOOK, YOU BEEN HOODWINKED, YOU BEEN BAMBOOZLED!"

I could go further but there is no need. I think by now you see the point. There are many ways in which people are foolish to fall in love. In actuality people have been sold a bill of goods. It's like Malcolm X once said, "You been took, you been hoodwinked, you been bamboozled." People don't know any better and sadly, people also don't know that there is another way.

People have been so conditioned to act out 'falling in love' that they don't see how they are killing themselves mentally. They continue acting out the same drama over and over but nothing changes. How long does a person have to keep getting hurt before they get tired? How many marriages does a person need before realizing that there must be a better way? Aren't you tired of this on-again-off-again dynamic? If not you should be. All of the energy being used to chase a relationship, and then set it up to fail, let me repeat that—WE set it up to fail—could be used on something worthwhile like developing a cure for cancer or some other world-changing effect.

Don't get me wrong. I do not mean to imply that there is something wrong with relationships. Relationships are wonderful, and in many ways should be encouraged. What is wrong in relationships is our **IDEAS** and *PRACTICES* about them. A relationship is not going to make you happy. A relationship is not going to make you whole or make you complete. There is not something wrong with you if you are not involved in a relationship. All of these **ideas** lead to the disintegration of relationships and their premature failure.

ANOTHER WAY
(IDEA)

Is there another idea about relationships that is empowering? Why continue to create hurt and agitation for yourself? If you look at the vast majority of relationships, isn't hurt and agitation that which you see? If you don't see this in your relationship, look at others around you. It is a pretty common and recurring theme. What if you and your potential mate—prior to seriously dating—decided that the both of you were going to help each other discover the hidden aspects of each other—baggage—so that those could be turned into positives. What if people's **ideas** about relationships shifted to having it looked at as a means for discovering aspects of yourself that you did not know were there previously? What if people's **ideas** about relationships shifted to having it become a vehicle in which you help your mate become a better person? What if people's **ideas** about relationships shifted to having each person see their mate as a spiritual being and that each person was helping their mate develop the inner spiritual aspect of their being? What would happen? Over a small bit of time, a consciousness shift would occur. The impact of behavior on a person over a short period of time would lessen—in short, people would not get as upset about the underwear being left on the floor. Whether or not she put out would be less important since your seeing the spiritual aspect of your mate would unconsciously identify you with your mate's spiritual self. This consciousness shift would lessen the impact of one's feeling like something wrong is happening.

RELATIONSHIPS ARE MIRRORS WHICH ALLOW A PERSON TO SEE ASPECTS OF THEMSELVES THAT THEY DID NOT KNOW EXISTED. THEREFORE, THEY ARE A TOOL FOR SPIRITUAL GROWTH!

Relationships are the perfect vehicle for becoming better people. A mate is in fact a mirror for the other, and through the relationship, a person if they look gets to see themselves in a way that they don't see while single. This is a great opportunity to grow in all ways. When growth like this occurs, it becomes easy to live life spiritually, because you become less and less caught up in baggage that you did not know existed. Therefore you have fewer lenses to look through when looking at your mate and life itself.

118

I don't think for a moment that anyone wants to carry baggage that holds ultimately nothing but pain, frustration, hurt, rejection and all the other stuff. I simply do not believe this. We have it backwards folks! We go into relationships in a way that is designed to make us more hurt and more frustrated. Whether we like it or not, whether we face it or not, whether we bury our heads in the sand or not, once we become involved in a relationship **all** of our baggage is going to come to the surface.

When it arrives, we blame the other person, make them wrong, and immediately begin feeling bad. The situation can then go from bad to worse.

Why not accept that a relationship is going to bring up aspects of ourselves that we ourselves probably will not like. Why not do this in the context of being with a mate who wants to be with you, who is willing to work with you on those aspects. These aspects are called obstacles. They are obstacles to having a fulfilled relationship. They are obstacles to living a spiritual life. And if you allow them to be, they are obstacles to seeing what's right in front of you. A person that can help you and you help them become the highest form of person there is. A spiritual person having a human experience!

Why not develop a new mindset about relationships? Why not a new **idea**? Guess what you would get with a new approach? A mate who would be considerate of your shortcomings since the relationship would be founded upon the recognition that each person has them. Therefore you would immediately bring compassion into the relationship and simultaneously remove contempt. You would get a mate with a growing sense of patience with themselves and with you since they would realize that this new evolution would take time. You would get a mate who would grow spiritually with you and you with them. How is this so you may ask?

Because helping a person beyond their own obstacles helps the person grow beyond the dumb stuff that keeps people bogged down. This is what spiritual work is actually all about: helping a person grow beyond themselves.

A person really is not able to live a spiritual life when stressed, frustrated, hurt, angry, resentful, lonely, and the host of other things that people feel in a relationship. Helping a person eliminate the child-like baggage that makes people respond in the hurt, frustrated, and so on ways is really the purpose for a relationship. It is also the key towards putting a person on the path to living their entire life 24/7 in a spiritual way.

AN "ETERNAL LOVE" IS THE ONLY TYPE OF LOVE THAT TRULY EXISTS. IT IS "LIVE" NOT "MEMOREX." ANY OTHER TYPE OF LOVE IS A SET-UP FOR FAILURE

What else happens in this process? A different type of love develops. A deeper one. As you begin to see the spiritual aspect of your mate on a regular basis, your love for them grows beyond the outer exterior of the person, their body. You grow to love the higher aspect of them. Their soul. You know that the soul itself is eternal. Therefore, as you begin to love the soul in your mate, the love that develops becomes an eternal one. This love of the soul is a love that people in this society do not experience. Frankly it is not possible to achieve this type of love the way relationships are practiced in this society.

Who wouldn't want an actual eternal love?

This type of love transcends the puppy-love drug addict type of love. It is the type of love that once perfected is always present. This type of love does NOT mean that a couple will always stay together. They may decide for whatever reason, that some day it is best for them split up. But this eternal type love always remains. Therefore, there is no bitterness at the time of breaking up or very little compared with break-ups of relationships during our era.

So again I ask, why in the area of romance do we continue to do the same things over and over again when clearly it is not working?

A new **idea** has been presented. A new way of thinking about relationships. This new **idea** can be used for a new couple or for a couple who have been together for awhile. It will work most effectively though in a new relationship, as this can be the foundation for the relationship to launch from. In a relationship that is already established, people may be to deeply entrenched in their positions of who is right versus who is wrong. If this is the case, it may actually be in a person's best interest to start all over again.

120

A great deal of psychological damage occurs in an unhappy relationship. For an older relationship, much patience, much time and much effort to practice this new way of thinking will be needed. This extra effort may not be something both people want, when they are entrenched in their views of who is right and who is wrong.

Maybe this new **idea** of relationships may not be something you agree with. If not, develop a new way of approaching a relationship for yourself, see if your potential mate buys into it, and then the both of you develop your relationship around this new ideal.

When a new **idea** about relationships is fostered and developed, it is at that time that relationships will become actual vehicles for a love that will promote the spiritual development in a person. An eternal love. At this point you would no longer be a fool to fall in love. You would be foolish not to.

REFLECTION:

1   **Do the present *Ideas* and Practices on Relationships work?**
2   **Will they stand the test of time?**

CHAPTER 10

Sick & Tired of Being Sick & Tired
(Conclusion)

REFLECTION:

1   What happens when a person becomes Sick & Tired of being Sick & Tired?

2   People who live life based upon *mistaken Ideas* are living in an *illusionary world!*

Since I was young child, I'd heard that Sojourner Truth coined the saying "Sick and tired of being sick and tired." Whether these were her words or not, the meaning behind it is most certainly true as it describes a state that happens when you have reached your limit. You have had enough and can take no more.

The title of this chapter describes a state that happens when you have reached your limit. You have had enough and can take no more.

This state of mind is necessary before you can make real substantive changes in your life. You usually know that there are things that you should do for yourself and your well-being. Stop smoking; eat better; get more exercise for example.

But you won't make any solid changes until you reach the point where you too become sick and tired of being sick and tired. I knew of a man who smoked cigarettes all of his life. He tried to quit on several occasions but couldn't. On a regular office visit, he was told by his doctor that if he didn't stop smoking he would have to have one of his lungs removed. He stopped cold turkey! Suddenly he became "sick and tired of being sick and tired."

Many of us are stuck in the daily flow of life because we haven't yet reached the point of being "sick and tired of being sick and tired" about anything. Many simply exist and just get along. The only thing in their life that changes is the day of the week. If not for the calendar showing today is a different day from yesterday, NOTHING in that person's life changes: work at the same job, make the same complaints, wish for the same things, and settle for a tomorrow that looks a lot like today.

People think that they can solve problems with quick and easy solutions. This is a mistaken **idea**. People properly solve problems only *when they grow sick and tired of being sick and tired of having the problem*! Until then no substantive change will occur.

This means that people must first ADMIT they have a problem. This must happen whether a solution is known or unknown. Alcoholics are generally not allowed into Alcohol Anonymous (AA) meetings until they admit that they have a problem. AA meetings have what is known as a twelve step solution to help one recover from the ravages of alcoholism.

What are people's problems? People as a whole think they are human beings having intermittent spiritual experiences instead of the opposite. Many people also are subject to every whim of their senses. Therefore, they do not have absolute control over their lives. They are not in control of their life. Their ego is.

Solutions are not what are needed. ACCEPTANCE of the fact that there is a problem is what is needed. Solutions mean little to a person who does not recognize that they have a problem. Solutions mean little to a person who has not yet reached the point where they are sick and tired of being sick and tired of having a particular problem. This fed-up feeling is VERY important. This feeling acts like a fuel and gives a person the strength to overcome the problem. Strength—fuel—is necessary as tackling internal issues takes time and much effort.

Not everyone is seeking the answer to what I consider to be the ultimate question in life, "Who Am I?" However, many if not all would like to take absolute charge and control over their life. The material as presented is like a map that if followed will guide one to the answer of either question. However, a map means little if you do not follow it.

People have asked why the material in this book doesn't give the reader a specific solution to the subject matter as presented. This was done purposely. As stated previously, solutions don't help people who have not yet admitted they have a problem. Solutions do not help people who are not yet sick and tired of being sick and tired of a particular circumstance, issue, or way of thinking.

However, this realization is actually the first part of solving your problems! We think that we can change behavior by finding the 'right' solution. That's like thinking you'll live happily ever after once you find the 'right' person. It doesn't happen like that. So although a step-by-step solution is not found in this volume, (you will have to wait for volume two) the most important part of the solution is given here: when you recognize which **ideas** are mistaken, you will be so fed up (sick and tired of being sick and tired) with the mistaken **idea** that you will be ready to find a real and lasting solution.

People are addicted to living life based upon *mistaken* **ideas**. This addiction is no different from that of an alcoholic. It is very easy to live life from an automatic-pilot status. There is nothing to do or think about when the automatic pilot is in control. No mental or physical effort is required when the automatic pilot is flying the plane. Just watch the instrument panel, (eat) check the pressure, (sleep) make some announcements to the passengers, (talk to family and friends) and there is nothing to do.

It takes mental and physical effort to fly a plane manually. A single mistake could be a disaster. But flying a plane on your own is scary. There is no one else to blame if something goes wrong.

Fear can make it hard to think for yourself—to stop living life based on *mistaken* **ideas**. It is fear that makes it hard to control yourself. Fear leads us to want to be like everyone else. We are afraid of making a mistake and having no one to blame but ourselves.

Every day you meet people who appear to be happy and contented. Outwardly, they appear like they have everything together. But internally, many people are unhappy and insecure. Many do not like themselves. Some people use illegal and legal drugs as a way to escape from a negative opinion of themselves. Some use alcohol. But there are other ways people seek shelter from the negative-insecure-aspect of themselves. People often hide from themselves by blending in and becoming one in the crowd. By doing what everyone else does…by turning a *mistaken* **idea** of the masses into reality.

Are you ready to critically look at the areas in your life in which you are living based upon an **idea** given to you by society? An **idea** that upon reflection is not true? Are you ready to actually think for yourself about every aspect of yourself? Totally? Do you have what it takes to be totally responsible for EVERY aspect of your being?

Then first recognize that you, like the alcoholic, must admit that you are addicted to living life according to *mistaken* **ideas**. Second, you must evaluate every area in your life in which you are living with someone else's **idea**. Then you must ask yourself if you are sick and tired of being sick and tired of not being totally responsible for yourself. Have you had enough? Does the thought—the smell—of allowing others to control your concept of reality make you sick?

For those who are sick and tired of being sick and tired about others controlling your concept of reality, the following must be done before you will be ready for the solution. The solution which will be given in the next book. Every *mistaken* **idea** that you base a substantive part of your life on is a separate addiction. So you should reflect on the different areas of your life and recognize what **ideas** are driving you.

This will take awhile. It will not occur overnight. People have practiced their particular way of living life for all of their life. Introspection of every aspect of ones' self if done critically will take time. Determining if one is sick and tired of being sick and tired for each aspect requires undisturbed thought and reflection.

While all of this reflection is done consider the following.

There was a time when the Queen of England was known as the cleanest person in the land. She bathed approximately twice a year. This was the *mistaken* **idea** of the time about cleanliness and personal hygiene. This lack of hygiene contributed greatly to the plagues that ravaged Europe. Today it is hard to believe that anyone thought or lived like this. At the time, everyone acted in accordance with this *mistaken* belief. In sum, this **idea** was the reality of the people. This so-called reality was an ***illusion.***

There was also a time when the medical community in the United States thought that the use of heroin could be used as cough medicine. This *mistaken* **idea** was so entrenched in the nation that in 1898 the Bayer Drug

Company marketed heroin as a non-addicting cough medicine. Everyone today knows that heroin is anything but non-addictive. No one today would take it for relief from a cold either.

These are additional examples of *mistaken* **ideas** that were untrue at a time but were believed and acted upon by the people. These *mistaken* **ideas** were accepted as true. The acceptance of these false **ideas** as real made them obstacles to living a spiritual life. Obstacles to answering the question *Who Am I?* Obstacles to taking control and charge of your life.

Unfortunately, time is generally required to show people the reality of a *mistaken* **idea**. Are you willing to wait one hundred years to find out that one of your outlooks on life was based upon an **idea** that was not true? Since people do not generally live to be more than one hundred years old, one may die not ever knowing that they lived a part of their life based upon an **idea** that was mistaken. This may be ok if you are mistaken about one or two aspects. What if you your entire way of being is based upon a *mistake*? One could live an entire lifetime based upon an ***illusion,*** die and never know otherwise. What a waste of life! Why put your life in the hands of others? If anyone should make a mistake, it should be you while in the process of seeking that which is true.

The **ideas** and *practices* addressed in each of the previous chapters constitute a person's perception of what they consider reality to be. The entire "whole" perception is made up of the sum of its parts. Each chapter presented an aspect of life, which is a "part" of the "whole." There are other aspects of life that were not addressed in this book. Sex, religion, success, and contentment to name a few. There are hosts of others. However, reflection on the topics addressed gives the reader a means of understanding their present **ideas** about reality and where they come from.

The nine chapters or ways of thinking presented in the book are obstacles to living a spiritual life. Obstacles to answering the question "Who Am I." Obstacles to taking control of your life. These ways of "seeing" life give people a sense of reality that is false. These obstacles give people a sense of reality that is in fact an illusion.

The misperception of reality is not confined to specific types of people or groups. It does not matter if you are single or married, young or old. It does not matter if you adhere to a specific system of study or if you do not. It does not matter if you are Agnostic, Muslim, Christian, Buddhist, Hindu, Jewish, Neterian or whatever. If you live life or practice your teaching with a mindset of **ideas** and *practices* that are not based upon truth, then you are living in a world of illusion.

It can be argued that the greatest thinkers of today are scientists. This group is not afraid to let everyone know that in the world of science, **ideas** about so-called truths are lucky to last ten years. In the scientific world, reality changes at minimum every ten years. Science changes as knowledge increases. It grows and evolves. It does NOT stay the same!

However, single and groups of people rarely change based upon growth and evolution. People may physically grow older but often their thoughts remain the same. Hence, the term, "this is the way I am, the way I have been, and the way I will always be." In the realm of thoughts and thinking, people as a whole choose to continue believing that the world is flat.

You must realize that it is *YOU* who are responsible for every aspect of your life. *YOU* must realize that *YOU* created your present circumstance based upon *YOUR* previous actions and thoughts. *YOU* must recognize that *YOU* can create something different. If this is not done, then *YOU* will never *identify* with the aspect of yourself that is mighty and great. *YOU* will never be able to exhibit faith like a mustard seed, act on that faith, and develop a will power that will bring things into being based upon that faith. *YOU* will create a victim mentality and live in accordance with that mentality. *YOU* will see yourself as being at the effect of life and not the cause of it. One who talks faith, but one who is actually afraid to act on it. Without this realization, *YOU* will not be able to fully understand the subtle aspects of whatever philosophical or religious doctrine you study. The authors of the entire world's religions and philosophies had a much different idea about who *YOU* are than is generally accepted. A much different **idea** about who one is innately and what one should be doing in life.

YOU must realize that the present *idea practiced* about Love is not the same as that which is described in the books of the masters. *YOU* can now see that your concept of Love is allowing *YOU* and society to do the opposite of Love. The opposite is hate. The present concept on Love creates an environment in which people condone the misapplication of justice. This environment also condones the misappropriation of the world's resources

127

into the hands of the few at the expense of the many. The Love practiced today allows one to see others as enemies. People outside of ones' "special classification of people" easily become enemies. Once an enemy, society condones and justifies their mistreatment and killing. With this *mistaken* **idea** of Love, *YOU* will not be able to identify with the type of Love that is actually being espoused in the tradition of study that you practice. Love is a many splendid thing that is to be given to ALL, not just to the few. True Love does not look like what is called Love today. True Love gives much and requires nothing in return. True Love, is that which Loves ALL without discrimination and without fail because one becomes Love. This is the **idea** about Love that has been written about and described throughout the ages.

YOU must realize that intermittent Happiness is not happiness at all. Intermittent happiness creates pain and suffering. The **idea** that happiness is intermittent is an **idea** which is false. Happiness is a birthright. Happiness was designed to be perpetual. Anything other than perpetual happiness is an *illusion*.

YOU must realize that *YOU* cannot continuously put pesticides, chemicals and other harmful things into your body without suffering repercussions. *YOU* must realize that the mind is fed daily whether *YOU* consciously feed it or not. A constant diet of violence, sex, murder, jealously, envy, anger, and greed will not assist one in answering the question "Who Am I?" It will not allow you to take control of your life. *YOU* must realize that the soul needs to be fed and its proper food is through meditation. *YOU* must realize that proper foods for all three aspects of the being are necessary to achieve COMPLETE FULFILLMENT.

YOU must realize that as long as *YOU* choose to remember a so-called wrong done to *YOU* by another, forgive but not forget, then *YOU* have bought in to the *make believe reality* of the ego. *YOU* have chosen to be a victim. Only the ego can be hurt. *YOU,* the real you is much more than an ego.

YOU must recognize that everything you do on a consistent basis is a practice of that thing. This means that one becomes good at those things they do the most often. *YOU* cannot "talk" about living life to the fullest while consistently practicing being frustrated, disappointed, jealous, and angry and the whole gamut of emotions. If *YOU* profess belief in a particular philosophical or religious doctrine and *YOU* do not live by its teachings

EVERY DAY at ALL TIMES, then you are unconsciously becoming an expert in that which is contrary to that which you profess.

YOU must realize that you are NOT the skin organ. *YOU* must recognize that you are not the common conception of what people consider a human being to be. *YOU* are not a human being having intermittent episodes of spiritual experiences. This idea is incorrect. It is the opposite. *YOU* ARE actually a spiritual being having an intermittent human experience! Until this mistake is corrected, *YOU* will have an altered view of what it means to be human and to have a soul. Without this understanding, *YOU* will not be able to *fully* identify with the teachings as espoused by Krishna, Jesus, Prophet Muhammad (P.B.U.H.), Buddha, and All of the Sages and Saints of Ancient Egypt related to life generally and the soul specifically.

YOU must recognize that society's present ideas about Relationships are skewed and actually create the environment for a 50% divorce rate for first time marriages and 60% divorce rate for seconds. Following the present societal **ideas** about relationships sets them up to fail. *YOU* must recognize that all people have emotional "baggage" that they bring with them into a relationship. Failure to address this baggage at the beginning of the relationship leads to its downfall. *YOU* must realize that relationships allow people to come to grips with aspects of their personality that they are not aware of. It is these aspects of one's personality that need to be addressed so that they can be strengthened. A relationship *premised* on the realization that both people have baggage allow both partners to help each other strengthen negative aspects of their personality from a place of Love. Many relationships deal with "baggage" from a place of criticism, anger, and upset ness. "Seeing" your mate as a "spiritual being" literally at all times without fail is a new **idea** which allows one to be compassionate and patient when helping ones' mate strengthen a negative or weak aspect of their personality.

Upon reflection, it is clear that people's **ideas** about life come from society and culture. They are NOT **ideas** that people consciously chose. People in many instances have forgotten that they have the ability to live life based upon an **idea** that may contradict the societal view. As stated previously, at one time people thought the world was flat. At one time, some people thought it was appropriate to bathe once or twice a year. These ideas in hindsight have been proven to be totally incorrect. What are **YOUR** ideas about personal responsibility, love, happiness, nutrition and forgiveness? What are the practices that **YOU** do on a daily basis which reinforce those

ideas? Which one/s will last for ten years? Fifteen years? Fifty years? Will these **ideas** be laughed at in the future like the **idea** that the world is flat would be laughed at today?

Are you now willing to look at the **ideas** in this book and others not mentioned critically, and choose to keep **ideas** that match with YOUR view of life and discard those that contradict it? **Ideas** that will help YOU answer the question "Who Am I". **Ideas** that will allow **YOU** to take charge and control of YOUR life. Will **YOU** then act in accordance with this critical analysis, or will you act like the masses of people that would rather have the automatic pilot fly the plane?

Keep in mind at all times that it is your **ideas** and **thoughts** that shape and create your reality. The sages, saints, authors, and founders of all religions had a much different *"idea"* about life and its purpose than the present society. They had much different *"practices"* which reinforced those ideas. *Ideas and Practices* that lead you to the answer of the question. Once the discovery of this **idea** is made, the answer to the question "Who Am I" will follow in a short time.

REFLECTION:

1   How many areas in YOUR life are based upon *mistaken* Ideas?
2   Have YOU been living YOUR ENTIRE LIFE in a make-believe world? A world of *illusion?*

Peace and Blessings!

ACKNOWLEDGEMENTS

I WISH TO ACKNOWLEDGE MY DAUGHTER NAILAH WHO HAS ALWAYS BEEN MY BIGGEST FAN. THE ONE WHO THOUGHT THAT HER FATHER COULD DO ANYTHING.

MY APPRECIATION ALSO TO DEBBIE N., WHO GAVE ME THE SUGGESTION OF USING THE WRITTEN MATERIAL, DEVELOPED FOR OTHER REASONS AS A MANUSCRIPT FOR THIS BOOK. TANYA S., WHO READ THE EARLIEST VERSION OF THE MANUSCRIPT AND HELPED KEEP ME FOCUSED ON MY TARGETED AUDIENCE. HEATHER T., CONNIE F. (SESHETA), AND JUDY C. (AMUNYT) WHO ALSO READ THE MANUSCRIPT AND PROVIDED ME WITH VALUABLE ADVICE.

FINALLY, I WISH TO ACKNOWLEDGE THE PRESENCE WHICH IS KNOWN BY MANY NAMES BY DIFFERENT GROUPS OF PEOPLE. ALLAH, BUDDHA, CONSCIOUSNESS, DIVINE, GOD, JEHOVAH, JESUS, KRISHNA, NEBERDJER, YAHWEH. IT IS THIS SAME PRESENCE KNOWN BY MANY NAMES WHICH HAS ALLOWED THIS WORK TO COME FORTH.

A NOTE ABOUT
THE AUTHOR

LAWRENCE R. MATHEWS WAS BORN AND RAISED IN DETROIT, MICHIGAN. HE IS THE FIRST IN HIS IMMEDIATE FAMILY TO GRADUATE FROM COLLEGE, COMPLETING HIS STUDIES AT WESTERN MICHIGAN UNIVERSITY IN 1986. HE RECEIVED A BACHELOR OF BUSINESS ADMINISTRATION, B.B.A. DEGREE. HE IS ALSO THE FIRST TO ATTEND GRADUATE SCHOOL, COMPLETING HIS STUDIES AT MICHIGAN STATE UNIVERSITY DETROIT COLLEGE OF LAW IN 1996. HE RECEIVED A JURIS DOCTOR, J.D. DEGREE.

MR. MATHEWS WORKED AS AN EDUCATOR FOR THE DETROIT PUBLIC SCHOOLS FOR APPROXIMATELY EIGHT YEARS AND AS AN ATTORNEY FOR NINE YEARS. HE HAS PRACTICED BEFORE THE MICHIGAN SUPREME COURT, THE MICHIGAN COURT OF APPEALS, AND HAS HAD MORE THAN 25 JURY TRIALS MAINLY AS A CIVIL DEFENSE ATTORNEY.

MR. MATHEWS OTHER INTERESTS INCLUDE THE PRACTICE OF YOGA, MEDITATION, AND VEGETARIANISM. HE ALSO STUDIES ANCIENT RELIGIONS. HE IS CURRENTLY A PRACTIONER OF EGYPTIAN YOGA AND A STUDENT AND PRACTICING YOGI AT THE SEMA INSTITUTE AND UNIVERSITY OF YOGA IN MIAMI, FLORIDA.

FOR MORE INFORMATION ON THE UNIVERSITY GO TO: HTTP://WWW.EGYPTIANYOGA.COM

MR. MATHEWS BELIEVES THAT EVERYONE IS SEARCHING FOR THE SAME THINGS IN LIFE: HAPPINESS, PEACE, JOY AND CONTENTMENT. THESE CAN BE ACHIEVED BY EVERYONE PERPETUALLY ONCE IT IS REALIZED THAT THESE CHARACTERISTICS MUST BE PRACTICED. PEOPLE ARE FRUSTRATED,

ANGRY, AND UNHAPPY BECAUSE PEOPLE PRACTICE THESE BEHAVIORS EVERYDAY. *PRACTICE MAKES PERFECT* SO ONCE PEOPLE REALIZE WHAT IT IS THAT THEY PRACTICE EVERYDAY, THEY WILL THEN BE IN A POSITION TO PRACTICE SOMETHING ELSE THAT WILL CREATE FOR THEMSELVES A NEW REALITY.

ISBN 0-9786346-0-8

THE "PRACTICE" OF NETERIANISM

THE TERM NETERIANISM IS DERIVED FROM THE NAME "SHETAUT NETER." "SHETAUT" AS THE FIRST WORD MEANS *SECRET* OR *HIDDEN* OR *MYSTERY*. "NETER" AS THE SECOND WORD MEANS **DIVINITY**. "SHETAUT NETER" THEREFORE MEANS THE TEACHING ABOUT THE SECRET, HIDDEN "SUPREME BEING," OR "DIVINE MYSTERIES."[3]

WHAT IS SHETI?

SHETI COMES FROM THE ROOT WORD "SHETAUT" WHICH IS ABOVE WHICH MEANS **SECRET, HIDDEN, OR UNKNOWN** OR THAT WHICH CANNOT BE SEEN THRU OR UNDERSTOOD. SOMETHING WHICH IS A **SECRET** OR **MYSTERY.**

SHETI THEREFORE ARE THE *PRACTICES* AND *DISCIPLINES WHICH* LEAD A PERSON TO "*DISCOVER*" THAT WHICH IS *HIDDEN, SECRET,* OR *UNKNOWN* WHICH IS THE *UNDERLYING BASIS* OF ALL OF CREATION.

WHAT ARE SHETI "PRACTICES?"

ANY PRACTICE OR DISCIPLINE WHICH HELPS A PERSON DISCOVER THAT WHICH IS "HIDDEN" AND "SECRET" IS A SHETI PRACTICE. INHERENT IN THE PRACTICE HOWEVER IS THE UNDERSTANDING THAT A PERSON'S IGNORANCE OF THEIR HIGHER NATURE AND SELF IS AN IMPEDIMENT TO KNOWING THAT WHICH IS "HIDDEN." TO UNDERSTAND THE TEACHINGS WHICH ALLOW A PERSON TO "KNOW" THAT WHICH IS "HIDDEN" REQUIRES THAT A PERSON'S MIND/EGO BECOME PURIFIED OR CLEANSED. BOTH MUST BE PURIFIED AND CLEANSED OF THE CONSCIOUS, SUBCONSCIOUS AND UNCONSCIOUS IMPRESSIONS THAT HAVE A PERSON BELIEVE THAT

---

[3] For a detailed exposition of Neterianism see the book Egyptian Mysteries Volume 1 Shetaut Neter by Sebai Muata Ashby

THEY ARE SOEMTHING OTHER THAN THE TRUTH. MOST PEOPLE BELIEVE THAT THEY ARE PHYSICAL BEINGS HAVING INTERMITTENT SPIRITUAL EXPERIENCES. HOWEVER, THE OPPOSITE IS IN FACT THE TRUTH. WE ARE SPIRITUAL BEINGS HAVING AN INTERMITTENT PHYSICAL EXPERIENCE! UNTIL THERE IS A CERTAIN LEVEL OF CLEANSING OF THE CONSCIOUS, SUBCONSCIOUS AND UNCONSCIOUS IMPRESSIONS THAT HAVE US BELIEVE WE ARE THE BODY, THE ABILITY TO "FULLY" UNDERSTAND THE DEEPER ASPECTS OF THE TEACHING WILL BE LIMITED. SHETI PRACTICES ARE THEREFORE THE MEANS BY WHICH THIS CLEANSING/PURIFICATION OCCURS. IN OUR TRADITION, THERE ARE FOUR MAIN DISCIPLINES WHICH MADE UP AND CONSTITUTED THAT WHICH WAS KNOWN AS THE "MYSTERIES." THE MYSTERIES ARE WHAT WAS TAUGHT IN THE TEMPLES OF KEMET. THEY ARE THE **SHETI OF DEVOTION, SHETI OF MEDITATION, SHETI OF WISDOM,** AND **SHETI OF ACTION (MAAT).**

WHAT ARE THE DISCIPLINES RELATED TO THE SHETI "PRACTICES"?

BEFORE DISCUSSING THE DISCIPLINES RELATED TO THEM, IT MUST BE CLEARLY UNDERSTOOD THAT THE SAGES OF KEMET TAUGHT THAT THE EGO/PERSONALITY OF ALL PEOPLE IS COMPOSED OF THE FOLLOWING:

1. INTELLECT.
2. EMOTIONS.
3. WILL.
4. PHYSICAL BODY.

THEY BELIEVED THAT EACH ASPECT OF THE EGO/PERSONALITY CREATES CONSCIOUS, SUBCONSCIOUS AND UNCONSCIOUS IMPRESSIONS IN THE MIND WHICH AFFIRM AND REAFFIRM THE BELIEF THAT PEOPLE ARE THE "BODY." EACH SHETI PRACTICE WAS DESIGNED TO PURIFY/CLEANSE THAT SPECIFIC ASPECT OF THE PERSONALITY/EGO. THE SIMULTANEOUS CLEANSING OF EACH ASPECT WAS/IS KNOWN AS THE "INTEGRATED PRACTICE OF YOGA."

A. SHETI OF WISDOM (INTELLECT)

THE SHETI OF WISDOM IS THE PROCESS OF STUDYING THE HIGHEST TEACHINGS, (THE WISDOM TEXTS AND WRITINGS OF SAGES AND SAINTS) AND THEN REFLECTING AND MEDITATING ON THEM. THIS SHETI PRACTICE PURIFIES/CLEANSES THE "INTELLECT" OF IMPRESSIONS THAT THE BODY AND THAT WHICH APPEAR TO BE REAL THROUGH THE SENSES IS THE FULLEST EXTENT OF CREATION.

B. SHETI OF DEVOTION (EMOTIONS)

EVERYONE HA S A NEED TO LOVE AND BE LOVED. THIS OFTENTIMES MANIFESTS THRU US BY WAY OF OUR EMOTIONS. ANYONE WHO HAS EVER FALLEN IN LOVE IS AWARE THAT THERE IS A LOT OF ENERGY INVOLVED IN THIS STATE OF BEING. WHEN IN LOVE, PEOPLE SOMETIMES CANNOT EAT, SLEEP OR EVEN DRINK BECAUSE THEY ARE THINKING ABOUT THAT SPECIAL PERSON OR OBJECT OF THEIR AFFECTION. PHYSIOLOGICALLY MANY CHANGES OCCUR IN THE BODY. THE HEART RATE, BLOOD PRESSURE, AND OTHERS CHANGE WHEN A PERSON HAS THIS "FEELING." UNFORTUNATELY, NEGATIVE IMPRESSIONS ARE FORMED IN THE MIND WHEN A PERSON SEEKS LOVE FROM PEOPLE/OBJECTS IN THE WORLD. THE PERSON BEGINS TO THINK THAT THE PERSON/OBJECT (OR THE "*RIGHT PERSON OR OBJECT*") WILL MAKE THEM HAPPY.

WHAT IS NOT REALIZED BY PEOPLE IS THAT WHAT THEY ARE ACTUALLY BEING ATTRACTED TO IS THE "***HIDDEN, SECRET, UNKNOWN***" UNDERLYING ASPECT SPOKEN OF EARLIER IN THE PERSON THEY ARE IN LOVE WITH. IN EFFECT YOU ARE ATTRACTED TO THE "GOD/SELF" IN THEM WHICH YOU JUST SO HAPPEN TO BE BETTER AT SEEING IN THEM THAN IN OTHERS.

THE SHETI OF DEVOTION HAS AS ITS GOAL THE PURIFICATION OF THE EMOTIONS BY DIRECTING THIS ENERGY AWAY FROM THE "OUTER PHYSICAL BODY" OF A PERSON TO THE UNDERLYING BASIS IN THEM WHICH YOU ARE ACTUALLY ATTRACTED TO.

C.   SHETI OF MEDITATION (WILL)

EVERYONE HAS A WILL. THE PRACTICE OF MEDITATION STRENGTHENS THE WILL POWER OF A PERSON. THE PRACTICE ALSO CLEANSES THE SUBCONSCIOUS AND UNCONSCIOUS IMPRESSIONS IN THE MIND WHICH HAVE A PERSON BELIEVE THEY ARE THE BODY. IN THE ADVANCED STAGES, MEDITATION ALLOWS A PERSON TO "EXPERIENCE" THEMSELVES AS THE HIGHER ASPECT OF THEIR BEING.

D.   SHETI OF RIGHTEOUS ACTION

EVERYTHING THAT A PERSON DOES OCCURS THROUGH SOME TYPE OF ACTION. EVEN THOUGHTS THEMSELVES ARE ACTIONS. ALL ACTIONS ONCE PERFORMED LEAVE IMPRESSIONS IN THE MIND. IMPRESSIONS CAN BE LIKENED TO FEELINGS. YOU DO THIS ACT, YOU FEEL GOOD. YOU DO SOMETHING ELSE YOU FEEL BAD AND SO ON. HOWEVER MOST ACTIONS ARE DONE FROM THE PERSPECTIVE THAT WE ARE THE BODY. SO A CONSTANT CONFIRMATION OF US BEING A BODY IS GIVEN THRU OUR ACTIONS ON A SECOND BY SECOND BASIS.

THE SHETI OF RIGHTEOUS ACTION HAS A PERSON ENGAGE IN ACTIONS THAT HELP HIM/HER TO SEE THEMSELVES AS INFINITE, IMMORTAL ETC. THE RIGHTOUS ACTIONS IN OUR TRADITION ARE THE 42 PRECEPTS OF MAAT. LIVING YOUR LIFE ON A DAILY BASIS THRU THE "PRACTICE" OF THESE PRECEPTS WILL PURIFY THE EGO.